# WOMEN WHO KNEW
*The Mortal Messiah*

*SPECIAL FIRST EDITION*

Welcome to the special first edition of WOMEN WHO KNEW: *The Mortal Messiah.*

This book began as a Christmas program nearly seven years ago, and included three stories: Mary Magdalene at the tomb, the woman taken in adultery, and Christ's mother, Mary. (This program is still being performed around the country, and periodically I hear from people about it.)

Due to many requests, the other stories were written to complete this book over the next six months. And the path from there to here has been a long, often frustrating, and always faith-promoting one.

You are one of a limited number of people to receive this version. I hope reading it will help you to get into the Christmas spirit--the *true* spirit of Christmas: Christ, His birth, life and earthly ministry.

I hope you enjoy this book of my heart.

Heather Horrocks

# WOMEN WHO KNEW
## *The Mortal Messiah*

## Heather Horrocks

Word Garden Press
P.O. Box 27208
SLC, UT 84127-0208

www.womenwhoknew.com


ISBN 0-9748098-0-2

Printed in the United States of America
Alexander's Digital Printing, Lindon, Utah

For ordering information, go to back page.

WORD GARDEN PRESS
P.O. BOX 27208
SALT LAKE CITY, UTAH 84127-0208


SPECIAL FIRST EDITION December 2003
10 9 8 7 6 5 4 3 2 1

COVER PICTURE COURTESY OF
www. yesholyland.com

*Dedicated to
all God's children
who seek
to know Christ.*

# ACKNOWLEDGMENTS

First I must thank my Heavenly Father. This book, from beginning to end, has been a walk in faith for me. My hope is that this book be pleasing to my Lord.

I would like to extend my appreciation to George Kahlil of www. yesholyland.com for his very generous sharing of his picture of a first century AD Samarian lamp for use on the cover (and for his knowledge of ancient lamps, saving me from using the wrong one).

Thanks to Diane Stoddard and Kristin Holt, two of the best critique partners on the planet. I treasure your insightful red marks, your moral support and your happiness at my milestones.

Thanks to Sherry Lewis and Deloy Barnes. Your help was invaluable when I wrote the first version. We shared many good times.

Thanks to Valerie Holladay for your belief in the book and your desire to see it in print.

Thanks to Lani King, for suggesting so many of the beautiful songs to accompany the stories in the program.

Thanks to Wendy Jensen for sharing the Master Mender tickets with Valerie Brown, and to Valerie for passing them on to me--delightful serendipity.

Thanks to those who have helped me on the path of learning to write, especially Kathy Lloyd Jacobsen (your class was great!) and Dwight Swain

Thanks to my "cold readers"--Valerie Brown, Joan Swain, Pam Benson, Kathleen Wright, Allen Richardson, and Lynn Bright. You helped me refine the writing before I sent it off and I appreciate your insights. Thank you, Lynn, for the gift of the beautiful book.

Thanks to Chantel and Kaylee Stoddard for sharing your oil lamps.

This has truly been a group effort, and I could not have done it without any of you. Especially my family...

Thanks to my son, Patrick, for many hours of help.

Thanks to Christopher and Stephanie Barnhurst for burning the midnight oil to help me and for the offer of future help (I'll be taking you up on that!).

Thanks to all my moms and dads, especially my mother, Loya, through whom the Lord passed on my talent and who has been helping from the "other side."

Thanks to my children and step-children, my wonderful daughters-in-law and son-in-law, and my delightful grandchildren. It's finally here--a book on the shelf with my name on it and a witness of Christ that I would like to share with all of you.

Thanks to my sisters, September and Skye, for all the encouragement you have given me over the years. Your delightful card said it best, September: If sisters were flowers, I'd pick you both again.

And, most importantly, I thank you, Mark, for being there for me in so many ways: editing, fixing dinners, being my reality check, talking through stories, dealing with me on a deadline. I truly could not have started or completed this project without your help. I cherish your strength, your support, your caring, and your love--and the cool way you have of nudging me right through my fears into the "horrible, wholesome" sunlight beyond.

# TABLE OF CONTENTS

PREFACE
xi

\* \* \*

✳ ✳ ✳

# PREFACE

These stories are of actual women who lived on Earth during the Savior's life and ministry. I have worked to keep the stories scripturally and historically accurate. Of necessity, these stories have been fictionalized. It must be that way, as some of the scriptural references are only a few sentences long, one a mere half sentence. The references to Pilate's wife and Anna the Prophetess are particularly brief. These stories are my interpretation of these scriptures.

I have presented these twelve stories in chronological order, so the entire book would be a picture of Christ's life and earthly ministry, from beginning to end, as seen through the eyes of these women.

Please know that if you find anything of beauty in these pages, it comes from our Heavenly Father.

I have spent much time reading and praying and pondering, as well as writing. As I have studied, I have grown to respect these women greatly.

What wonderful experiences they had. They directly experienced the healing power of Christ's Atonement. How wonderful it must have been to look into Christ's eyes. Imagine the love they must have seen there. When the Messiah laid His hands upon their heads and blessed them, what great power and love did they feel emanating from Him? When the Savior forgave them of their sins and healed them, body and soul, imagine the healing power that must have surged through their body. It is hard to imagine what they must have felt merely standing in His presence. These women did not have to imagine--they *knew*.

Reading the scriptures, we can feel Christ's great love and respect for the women He interacted with, respect that most men of that time period and culture did not extend to women. We need to understand that we, as modern women, deserve that same love and respect, for we are children of God. We need to realize the healing power inherent in The Atonement and realize that power is still here upon the earth. Christ's healing light still shines. Will miracles never cease?

Truly it is a miracle that any of us--then or now--may forsake our sins and be forgiven through the Atonement of our Lord and Savior, Jesus Christ. It is a miracle that we can be healed from the hurts that are done to us, that we can be made whole again.

It doesn't matter that Christ lived on the earth two thousand years ago, for He still lives today. His power to heal is as great now as if He still walked the earth, as though He placed His hands upon our brow and blessed us Himself, as if He looked into our eyes. We can be healed as surely as if we touched His hem in a crowd, as surely as though we washed His feet with our tears and were forgiven, as surely as though our loved one was raised from the dead.

Through Christ, we can be born again. From darkness into the blessed light of Christ. *Alleluia!* For unto us is born this night a Savior. The star still shines.

Wise men and women still seek Him. The light still heals.

I pray that the spirit and light of Christ may touch our hearts. That our testimonies, our witnesses of Christ, may grow stronger each day until they fill our hearts and souls. That we may become men and women who *know*--as long as there is a Savior, there is hope.

# WOMEN WHO KNEW
*The Mortal Messiah*

"For with God
nothing is impossible."

*(Luke 1:37)*

# TO PREPARE THE WAY

## *Elisabeth,*
## *Mother of John the Baptist*

I clear the table and wash it, then rinse the cloth and hang it to dry. When my husband, Zacharias, reaches for the small satchel which contains his mid-day meal, I touch his arm. I do not speak until he turns to look into my eyes. "Please stay with me," I say, "for I cannot bear to be alone this day."

He opens his mouth, and I see the concern in his eyes. He cannot speak, but raises an eyebrow in silent question. I have come to read these facial messages well, but I do not know how to express the fear and doubt I feel this day. I am not sure myself exactly what it is I fear.

Zacharias motions for the writing tablet. It is so cumbersome for him to use instead of speaking. But he questioned the angel Gabriel himself when he prophesied that I would conceive, and Gabriel struck him dumb because of his doubt. So he uses the tablet, and writes: *Why, my wife?*

"Someone is coming today. I have felt it all morning."

Zacharias wipes the slate and writes again: *You cannot hide yourself away forever from the world.*

I hold my words for a moment. It is true I have hidden myself since I conceived. Neither Zacharias nor

3

I could endure the ridicule from those who would disbelieve. Or even the curiosity of those who would want to see for themselves the woman well stricken in years who carries a babe in her womb. I have already suffered enough stares and whispers in my lifetime. I know my aged body has been made young again somehow, but I do not want to explain this to others. I do not want anything to mar this sacred experience and so I hide myself.

I run my hand over my bulging belly: Gabriel said I would conceive, and indeed I have. And who can fault my dear Zacharias for doubting? We are of an age that it should be our grandchildren bearing babes of their own. Surely others laughed at Abraham's Sarah of old when she was told in her advanced years that the time had come now to conceive? And here am I--nearly as aged as Sarah--and I, too, carry a child within my once-barren womb.

"It is not that I want to hide from this visitor," I say. But how do I explain a feeling to Zacharias which I cannot clarify for myself? He is trying so hard to be patient, but I know how anxious he is to see to his work in his fields.

I sigh. He will stay if I ask again but then he will pace, if only in his mind, and will likely be no comfort to me after all. Zacharias has much need to be out and about his business, to pack activity into his day and so distract himself from the silence within him. So I hand

4

him the satchel, force a smile and say, "Go, my husband. Attend to your duties."

He embraces me and kisses my cheek, then writes on the tablet again and hands it to me: *The Lord will bless and keep you, my wife. Be patient.*

While I watch him cross the fields, I blink back tears, for I have heard similar words before. As I prayed over the years, the answer came--not always when I wanted--but always it came: *Have patience and the time will come when you will receive what you desire in righteousness.*

What more righteous desire could I have had than to raise a child to honor and obey his God?

And so I waited, month after month, year after year, decade after decade, as, all around me, women conceived with no effort. Giggling newly-married girls, women with suckling babes already at their breast, women weary of childbearing--all able to do something I could not. All speaking aloud my reproach from the Lord. All wondering what sin brought this punishment upon me.

But why do they question thus? For even the harlots conceive!

Over and over I have received this assurance that if I would only have patience, the righteous desires of my heart would be realized. And when my childbearing years had passed, I wondered if the assurance meant that perhaps I would be given another's child to raise as my own, and within me a hope for such a child would war with the guilt that something would have to happen to another woman for me to gain her child.

For these past months since I conceived, my joy has been full. What has happened to me is a miracle. The Lord has taken away my reproach among men and before women. He is pleased with me. At last I am with child.

And my babe is not just any child, but a child of promise. I carry one of God's chosen within my womb. The angel said his name was to be John, and he would be filled with the Holy Ghost, even from his mother's womb.

*His mother.* I love the sound of those words--his mother. Truly I am a living witness that with God nothing shall be impossible.

Or am I? The cause of the doubt and fear I could not fully express to Zacharias now becomes more clear to me. Though I am six months with child, my babe has not yet moved. My doubt brings with it a pain more exquisite than that of my barren years. I shut my eyes as though that will shut out the pain as well.

I blink back a tear as I remember the condescending and judgmental way other women treated me in my youth. My heart aches as I relive all the gossip and pointing fingers from hurtful women who openly accused me of being unworthy of the Lord's favor. Sometimes, in my weaker moments, when my arms ached to hold a child of my own, I, too, wondered what I had done to earn the Lord's disfavor. I have done all

I could to walk upright before the Lord but I never knew why I did not conceive. Nor do I know now what I did differently to earn the Lord's favor. But now those hurts seem as nothing, when they are compared to this--to nearly receive my deepest desire and then to have it snatched from me.

When a tear trickles down my old cheek, I let it fall and watch it spill onto my belly where the babe rests. Why have I not felt movement within my womb? Will I not carry this child to fruition? Will this be yet another reproach from God?

I am confused and frightened, for if I do not know, I cannot rectify my mistakes. I wonder if the honor of bearing this special babe will be given to another more worthy than I. The pain of it cuts through me. Its familiarity makes it lose none of its strength. Indeed it grows stronger and more hurtful. More tears flow down my cheeks.

I kneel beside the table and pour out my soul to the Lord. Oh, please, my God, do not take this child from me. Losing this babe now would be more than I could bear. I do not have the strength to survive one more bitter disappointment.

Please, dear God, if it be a righteous desire of my heart to ask, let me know that I have not fallen from Thy favor. Let me feel this child move, for I can withstand anything, any gossip, any condescending looks, any fear, any pain, as long as I know I have not displeased Thee. But if it be not Thy will, if I am under reproach, please give me the strength to endure that which must follow.

The answer I receive is the same, yet different. The words flow into my mind and touch my heart. *Patience, my dear daughter. I had need to prepare you in the refiner's fire so you would be ready to fulfill your mission. I am pleased with your efforts.*

And then there is nothing more. As so often before, I do not understand.

With a sigh, I struggle to my feet, take up my pestle, and try to block out my pain with familiar tasks. I crush a handful of grain in the mortar, but my thoughts do not cease and my pain does not dim. As I work, I look out the window and catch a glimpse of a woman walking up the dusty road, still too far away to recognize.

Perhaps this is the one I sensed would be coming to my home. But I wish it were Zacharias returning instead. Yet even when he is here, he is not. I miss him as he was before. I miss the sound of his voice, the deep rumble of his laughter, the feeling of peace that envelopes me when he speaks to the Lord in prayer. There are moments when I fear I have lost both my husband and my babe.

Other women have friends to turn to for comfort and advice, but there is no woman who would not look at me in disbelief and question silently.

I blink back yet another tear and remind myself of the miracle. *With God nothing is impossible.* I remind myself of the prophecies which speak of John and say he comes to prepare the way for the Messiah. I do not know how long I am lost in my thoughts before a knock at the door stirs me. This must be the person I felt would come, perhaps the woman walking on the road, yet I am no more ready to face a visitor now than I was before. I pull my mantle about my shoulders to shade my face and my swollen tear-stained eyes, and to cover my belly. Today of all days I want no questions, either spoken aloud or silent.

I hesitate for a moment before the door. When I open it, I find my kinswoman, Mary, the daughter of the Persian Prince Nakeeb Shah, now converted and known as Jacob, and of Princess Anna of Jerusalem. She is so much younger than I, a woman barely past a child, yet an air of dignity surrounds her. Just seeing her here calms my heart.

Before I can motion for her to enter, Mary smiles gently and greets me, "Elisabeth, my beloved cousin."

At the sound of her quiet voice, the Holy Spirit washes through my body as though I were a garment being cleansed in a stream. My arms and legs tingle, warmth fills my bosom, and tears overflow. An energizing force fills my entire body and my babe leaps within my womb!

Instinctively, I touch my belly where my child resides.

My babe lives! My babe lives! Blessed be my God, who has heard my prayers and answered my cries.

*This* is that moment which God promised and of which the angel prophesied, when he said my babe would be filled with the Holy Ghost, even from his mother's womb. My womb.

And I marvel at the miracle of the Messiah Himself, and at the woman who has even greater honor than mine own, to carry the babe who will be the Messiah, the King, the Redeemer, who will deliver Israel from her enemies.

The Holy Spirit whispers to me that Mary carries the Messiah now within her womb. I remember that the prophet Isaiah spoke of the virgin who would conceive and bear a son--a more miraculous conception even than my own barren one. She is the virgin spoken of by the prophet Isaiah. My heart swells with joy, for now I know the Lord does not hold me under reproach, but He allows me to see His miracles.

Tears borne of the Holy Spirit continue to flow down my cheeks. As the Holy Spirit opens my mind, a vision unfolds before me even as Mary and my home fade from before my eyes.

I see my son as a man, healthy and tall. He cries out, "Repent ye: for the kingdom of God is at hand. One mightier than I cometh, the latchet of whose shoes I am not worthy to unloose." I see that many people believe his words and follow him.

I see my son standing in the River Jordan beside the Messiah, Himself. My son asks humbly, "I have need to be baptized of thee, and comest thou to me?"

I realize that for this moment was my son conceived, and for this must I prepare him. An awesome sense of this mission for which the Lord has prepared me for so many years fills me as I hear the Messiah answer, "Suffer it to be so now: for thus it becometh us to fulfill all righteousness."

His voice is full of power, yet gentle, and the sound of it works its way into my heart. The Messiah looks into my eyes. In this brief instant, a powerful love envelopes me, and wipes away my pain. A complete peace settles over me. The peace of the Christ.

After I watch my son baptize the Messiah, I see the Holy Ghost descend like a dove, and rest upon the Son of God, and the Holy Spirit burns so warmly within my bosom I feel I must burst into flame. I hear a voice--the very voice of God!--from heaven, piercing to the center of my soul: "This is my beloved Son, in whom I am well pleased."

The fire in my soul burns away my pain, my fear, and all my past hurts. Every accusation made through the years is gone. My soul continues afire as the vision fades and Mary appears before me once again.

For what purpose does Mary come to visit me, one whose doubts have been so strong and whose faith has been so weak? I do not know, but as I look on this young woman-child, who is most beautiful and fair above all other virgins, I find that, even as Zacharias cannot speak, I cannot hold my tongue but must pay homage to the mother of the Messiah, "Blessed art thou

11

among women, and blessed is the fruit of thy womb. And whence is this to me, that the mother of my Lord should come to me?"

I kneel, but Mary takes my hand and helps me rise. She hugs me carefully, clinging to me as if she has need of strength herself. I feel the same incredible love emanating from within her and recognize it as coming from the Christ child within her.

There is no doubt now that I am loved, for the Holy Spirit testifies to it through every fiber of my being. I embrace her for a long moment as my babe moves again within me.

My heart overflows with joy. The Messiah comes as was prophesied, to prepare the way for my salvation. And my son will prepare the way for Him. I am honored and awed by the privilege of training this son of mine to be ready for that moment I foresaw.

The Lord has taken away my reproach. I have been patient as He admonished, and He has kept His promise to me. And how much sweeter and more glorious is this moment for the waiting.

Hosanna! Hosanna! Blessed be the name of the Lord forever and ever!

"And Mary said,
Behold the handmaid
of the Lord;
be it unto me
according to thy word."

*(Luke 1:38)*

# THE MIRACLE
## *Christ's Mother, Mary*

Sweet Bartholomew (for that is the whimsical name I call our faithful old donkey) is as tired as I am. He has carried me for five days and never balked over the ninety mile trip. Sometimes, when my large body cramps and aches from sitting on his back for so long, I have asked Joseph to help me off and I walk alongside them.

But this afternoon I dare not, for my pains have begun. Please, Lord, let our journey be done this night for this babe comes soon. Please do not let this child of Thine be born alongside this dusty road.

The sun has beat down on me all day. Normally, Joseph would have stopped and let Bartholomew rest, but we can see Bethlehem from where we are and I can feel Joseph's urgency to get there. I have not said anything to him, but he knows.

The donkey stumbles and I pull tight on his mane to keep from falling. The movement causes another pain to begin. Each has become more surprising in its strength.

Please, Lord, help me this night. I am honored to be the sacred vessel for Thy child, but I am so frightened.

The sun has dipped low in the sky, and the desert's evening chill makes me shiver and pull my mantle about my shoulders. We are now passing by the first homes in Bethlehem. My pains have grown quite regular and when they come I have to catch my breath. When I do, Joseph stops the donkey and rubs my back until I can look at him and smile again. Worry creases his brow, and he walks much faster now, almost pulling Bartholomew along. He knows we have to find a place soon.

But we have stopped at three inns already. My pains are so strong. There--another one. I know from helping my mother that this can last a while, but I wonder how I can bear it. How strong will the pains become? Am I close now? Or do I have hours yet to go? There is no one to tell me.

Oh, how I wish my mother were here with me! I know the prophecy says the Messiah child will be born in Bethlehem, but at what cost to me? I am so tired and so frightened. Please, Lord, help me through this night.

Joseph comes back from the doorway of yet another inn. He is smiling, but I can tell it is forced. He tells me there is no room, but then hastens to add that the innkeeper has a place for us in back. He pauses. "In the stable."

"A stable?" I ask, disappointed. For God's son?

When I was still a child, I always planned to give birth in my own home, as my mother gave birth in hers, with other women around to assist. But I am far from home and I have only Joseph to help.

At least I do have Joseph, who has always loved me and has always trusted me. Even when word came to him that I was with child, and others said he must put me away, he could not do it publicly and did not want to do it at all. Even then, he prayed to the Lord to know what to do for he is a just man. Even before the angel gave him the reason for his trust, he has always trusted me.

Joseph walks the donkey around to the back of the stable. There are animals there. I try to hide my sigh as Joseph helps me down, but he hears me. As he walks me under the shelter, the air is warm inside. But how? Joseph says it is the heat from the animals. But I do not care, as long as it is warm. The animals watch us walk in, but they do not move.

Another pain begins, much stronger than the rest, and I begin to cry. How can I give birth in here? With no women to help? I love Joseph, but he is a man, and how much help can he be during childbirth? I am overcome with my fears.

Suddenly, I feel a peaceful warmth as someone comforts me. I look around, but I see no one but Joseph and the animals. Yet this is not the first time I have felt God's presence while I have carried His child, so I recognize this warmth as it fills my heart and I know God is with me this night to witness the birth of His son. Peace fills my soul as a great love surrounds me. Tears well in my eyes, for my prayers have been answered.

Joseph looks up with startled eyes and I know he has felt this same spirit, as well.

The next pain comes, but it is not so hard to bear as the others. I have angels for midwives, and I could ask for no better.

I thank thee, Lord, for the privacy and shelter this stable provides so I do not have to give birth alongside the dusty road.

I thank thee for these animals so the babe will not be chilled as He comes into this world.

I thank thee for my strong and loving Joseph, so I am not alone this night.

I thank thee for entrusting me with this sweet child, for I feel His strong presence already, along with Thine.

God's child is here, and He is beautiful. Unto us this night is born a Savior.

Joseph takes the baby in his large calloused hands and gently cleans Him and wraps Him in swaddling clothes. What an incredible man Joseph is that God would trust His son with him, not for this moment alone, but to instill the truth in Him and to be the footsteps for God's child to follow.

I did not think I could love Joseph more than I did before, but in this moment my love for him is so great it is almost painful.

As he gently places the baby into my arms and calls Him Jesus, I touch my fingers to the tiny, red, wrinkled face. I unwrap the swaddling clothes Joseph has so lovingly secured around Him so I can count ten fingers and ten toes. Thus reassured, I wrap Him again and look upon His beauty.

Joseph points into the heavens and whispers, "Behold."

I look up. Among the many stars, I see a new star in honor of God's son and know that God is well pleased, even as I feel God's spirit withdraw. Now I am alone with this child, but I am not alone because I know there are angels to watch over Him and I still have my beloved Joseph.

I look into this baby's eyes, and love fills me more than I ever thought possible and I know I would die for this child. He is *my* beloved son, as well.

I see knowledge and truth and the wisdom of the ages flicker in His eyes. Yet He is tiny and helpless and He needs me.

I know Our Father has many tasks for this tiny child to accomplish in the coming years. Tomorrow Jesus belongs to the world. Thank Thee, Lord, for this night when this babe is still mine. Soon enough I will have to share Him with those who would worship Him and those who would hurt Him. Joseph and I can keep Him safe for a time, but for how long I know not.

But this night I will not fear. This night He is *my* son, to hold as any mother holds her babe. I gaze with love upon His beautiful face and into His bright eyes.

My baby is here.

"And there was one Anna,
a prophetess..."

*(Luke 2:36-37)*

# BEHOLD
# THE LAMB OF GOD
## *Anna, Prophetess at the Temple*

My name is Anna, the daughter of Phanuel, of the tribe of Aser, and I am of a great age. I am past one hundred years old and so I am perhaps the oldest of those working in the temple. The privilege still brings tears to my weary eyes.

When I was but a young girl, I married, but was left a widow seven years later, and have not departed from the temple since that time. I have been privileged to see what the future holds, and to speak of such, and thus am I called a prophetess.

I serve slowly, but surely, by fasting and by prayer. Today I kneel on my well-used cushion in a chamber of the temple and pray, as I have done for the past eighty-four years, and thus I serve my God. As I pray, a thought flickers through my mind, not even a thought so much as an impression, that I should go into the courtyard of the temple. It is an odd thought, but I have been in the temple long enough to recognize the voice of the Holy Spirit.

But it will take me so long to work myself to my feet that I dismiss the thought and continue to kneel. I pray for the widows, the orphans, the lame and the lepers.

Again I feel I should go into the courtyard. I know not what there is to see there that I have not seen many times before, yet I will go, when my prayers are completed, for getting to my knees and rising again are difficult for me these days. So I continue to pray, now for the Messiah who has been promised and whose prophesied time has come.

My knees ache from kneeling, but I stay where I am. The feeling to go comes a third time, but now it is as if a voice speaks loudly within my head, and says "Go into the courtyard of the temple. Go now."

There is no ignoring or mistaking the message this time. God speaks to me through His Holy Spirit, and I must obey. It takes me long moments to struggle to my feet and I wait for the tingles, those that I get from kneeling so long, to leave my feet before I dare take a step. Slowly I leave the room and travel the length of the corridor.

As I near the main entrance to the temple, I place my hand against the wall and catch my breath. This same hallway which I moved through so easily in my youth now seems so long.

Taking one last deep breath and pushing away from the wall, I step outside and squint in the bright morning sun. Even after my old eyes adjust to the light, I can see only blurred figures below me. I put out my hand and let it rest on top of the low wall I often use to steady my steps, and I work my way slowly and carefully down. If the Lord needed someone in the courtyard soon, He would not have chosen me for I go so slowly that even I grow impatient with my pace.

Finally, I am led by the Holy Spirit down the stairs and straight ahead. In the center of the courtyard, I see Simeon. He is a just and devout man who, like me, waits for the consolation of Israel. The Holy Spirit has revealed to him a glorious promise that he should not see death before he has seen The Christ. And so he works here in the temple and waits, even as do I, though I have not received such a glorious promise as his.

But I cannot doubt the Lord, for in His wisdom and in the proper time all things He has promised will come to pass.

Before Simeon, with their backs to me, stand a man and a woman. The moment I catch sight of them, the Holy Spirit floods my body, sending an energizing force into my limbs. What is there about this couple that would be so important to the Lord?

The man holds a cage with two turtle doves inside. The couple must be here to offer a burnt offering and a sacrifice for sin. Usually a lamb is provided, but perhaps these people cannot afford a lamb. Yet they do not look so poor.

"Go to them," the Holy Spirit whispers.

I know not who they are, but I work my way slowly toward them. As I reach the side of the woman, I see what I could not see before. She holds a babe in her arms, wrapped in the shepherd's plaid and the royal blue swaddling clothes of the House of David. Ahh. The days of her purification must be over according to the law of Moses. It is written there, in the law of the Lord, that every male that openeth the womb shall be called holy to the Lord, and this couple brings their firstborn male to present him to the Lord.

Of a sudden, the Holy Spirit flows through me so strongly that I feel the strength of youth. It is as if I hear the Hosts of Heaven singing just to me. *Messiah*, they sing. *Savior. Redeemer. Son of God.*

I reach out and touch the babe's hand, and the Messiah closes his tiny fingers around one of my large gnarled ones. Tears make their way down my wrinkled and withered cheeks.

*Counsellor. Prince of Peace.* As Isaiah prophesied so many years ago. The sign. A virgin shall conceive and bear a son. *Immanuel. With Us Is God.* Truly He is with us now.

The virgin mother looks into my eyes and smiles and then speaks to Simeon. "I bring no lamb for the offering, for my son *is* The Lamb."

*The Lamb of God. Savior. The Mighty God. Alleluia*, the Hosts of Heaven sing, but no one else seems to hear them. Yet I shall sing this song of prophecy to others this day.

"Alleluia," I sing with them, and then I ask, "May I hold the babe?"

The mother smiles and nods her approval. When I reach out, my hands do not shake as they have grown to do. The Spirit has made me young and strong for this moment, for God wants no harm to come to His Son because of my body's weakness.

I hold the Savior of the world in my arms and gaze in awe on His tiny face. His eyes gaze into mine and intelligence shines within them. Then He smiles sweetly at me and raises His tiny hand up toward my face.

I have worked hard for so many years, and thus the Lord my God rewards my service. I am here to witness the Christ child, along with Simeon who was promised. God led me to the courtyard to hold His son in my arms. Alleluia. Praise God and His Son.

Simeon steps toward me. I can see on his face that he also knows the meaning of the woman's words and he knows this is the fulfillment of the promise he received. Perhaps he heard the singing, as well. "Give the child to me."

I turn and let Simeon take the babe from me. On this sacred day Simeon will perform all rites for this child and His parents according to the law of the Lord, as if He is an ordinary child. Even The Lamb of God must have the ordinances performed as decreed by His law.

Simeon looks at the babe, as I did. Never have I seen tears flow from his eyes, in all these years of serving here with him, but this day they do so freely.

He lifts the babe in his arms, blesses God, and says, "Lord, now lettest thou thy servant depart in peace, according to thy word, for mine eyes have seen thy salvation which thou hast prepared before the face of all people; A light to lighten the Gentiles, and the glory of thy people Israel."

The couple marvels at his words, and the Spirit continues to testify to me the truth of Simeon's words. Surely this child *is* the promised Messiah.

Alleluia, my heart sings. Alleluia. The Messiah is born and comes as promised. God answers my prayers. For such a time as this was I born--for this very moment have I served. My heart sings with my joy. And inspiration fills me with heavenly light. I shall speak of Him to all those who look for redemption. I shall prophecy of Christ on this day to all who listen. I shall share the message of the heavenly hosts.

The Lamb has come. *Alleluia.*

"...a well of water
springing up
into everlasting life."

*(John 4:14)*

# LIVING WATER

## *Samaritan Woman at Jacob's Well*

The women of Sychar do not go to the well at the sixth hour, when the sun is high in the sky, so I choose this time to go. I carry my water pot to get precious sustenance for my vegetables, for it is hot and they will parch without it. I have made three trips today, each when the women of the village are away, and will make more before the day is done.

I have been careful to avoid the others, yet as I approach the well, I am dismayed to find someone resting on the rocks in the shade of the trees. I cannot tell who it is, but my first instinct is to leave and return later. Because each day people judge me anew for choices others have made, the pain of their judgments weighs upon me. Therefore, I seek to avoid the company of others. I could bear this pain more easily if it were simply for the consequences of my own choices. These people judge me, but they do not know what went on in private. They could not.

As I approach the well, I wonder, as I often do, what is wrong with me. I have violated no law. I have betrayed no man. It is true I have borne no sons, and for that my husbands have put me away. One after another five husbands sent me away. And for this do I endure speculation from the tongues of others.

I have learned to expect no kindness from others. I have borne daughters who I can no longer call my own as they belong now to my former husbands. I have no home of my own nor worldly possessions. Nor friends with whom to share my thoughts. I even doubt God's love for me, and it has been months since I dared pray for fear God would turn from me, as well.

As I approach the rocks, I see the visitor is a man. He leans against the cool rocks of the well in the shade. He looks weary, as if he has traveled far. I can tell by his robes that he is a Jew, and this makes me even more uncomfortable. There has been enmity between Jews and Samaritans for far longer than I have lived so this man will not bother me. He will never speak to a Samaritan, and certainly not to a woman. He will not know my past, so I will only have to suffer his silent stares of animosity because I am a Samaritan, and not because five men have cast me aside. Thus I am reassured. A Jew will not detain me. I can draw my water and be gone before the other women return.

I continue to the well, entering the cool shade, always such a welcome respite from the heat of the day. Stepping onto the rocks surrounding the well, I lean over to draw water, ignoring this Jewish man.

But as I pour the water into my pot, this man speaks to me. "Give me to drink," he says.

I nearly drop my water pot in surprise. I cannot believe he has spoken to me, a Samaritan and a woman, and my amazement carries over into my voice. "How is it that thou, being a Jew, askest drink of me, which am a woman of Samaria? For the Jews have no dealings with the Samaritans."

The man leans back and smiles at me, a gentle, weary smile. If any other man smiled at me at the well, I would leave immediately, for I have had enough of troubles with men. Yet this man is different. There is a peace about him which I feel strongly, and his voice carries this peace in waves I can feel as he speaks. "If thou knewest the gift of God, and who it is that saith to thee, Give me to drink; thou wouldest have asked of him, and he would have given thee living water."

Living water? What does he mean? What does he want with me? I should ignore him. I should draw my water and hurry away before the other women return, but I do not. Will the women treat me any worse if they see me talking to a strange man? They are already so cruel to me. Yet they could carry the tale to Rashidi, and I do not want a problem with him, the man I love but the one I dare not enter into a marriage contract with. I cannot trust so fully ever again. And I cannot bear the loss of Rashidi, for I love him dearly. I dare not enter into a marriage contract with him, and thus I live in sin with him. And that makes final everyone's judgments against me.

If the women find me speaking with a man, they could carry tales. And if they find me speaking with a *Jewish* man, I sense I will regret it deeply. Yet something kind in this man's face compels me to tarry longer and speak with him.

31

"Sir, thou hast nothing to draw with, and the well is deep: from whence then hast thou that living water? Art thou greater than our father Jacob, which gave us the well, and drank thereof himself, and his children, and his cattle?"

There is a peculiar light in the man's eyes, even in the shade. I have a hard time looking away from his eyes, yet I know not why other than he has a great spirit about him.

I would not be surprised to discover he is a Rabbi. But what kind of Jewish Rabbi speaks with Samaritans? And with women? For no man--even a Samaritan man--has ever thus conversed with me in this manner nor with any other woman that I know.

He does not answer my question about Jacob. "Whosoever drinketh of *this* water," he says as he points to the well, "shall thirst again: But whosoever drinketh of the water that I shall give him shall never thirst; but the water that I shall give him shall be in him a well of water springing up into everlasting life."

In spite of my doubts, I am intrigued. Would that I had water which, once swallowed, causes one to never thirst again. Such water would mean that I would never have to come to the well again. I would never have to face the whispers of the other women as they hurry away when I arrive. I would never again see my shame reflected in the eyes of others or know my failings by the reactions of those around me. I would never thirst again, Rashidi would never thirst again and my plants would never thirst again.  Surely there can be no such water, yet if there is I desire it.  "Sir, give me this water, that I thirst not, neither come hither to draw."  I pause.  How will he produce that which does not exist?

"Go," he says, "call thy husband, and come hither."

How do I answer him?  I live with Rashidi, but he is not my husband.  I swore I would never again give a man the opportunity to hurt me as those others have done.

I have five parchments in my basket at Rashidi's home.  Most women never get even one Bill of Divorce and Deed of Release, yet I have five.  Well, I will not have six.  I love Rashidi as I have loved no man, and I still have need of a man to protect me, but how do I tell this man any of this?  How do I explain my shame or admit aloud my failings?  Finally, I settle for a half truth, "I have no husband."

He smiles again.  'Thou hast well said, I have no husband: For thou hast had five husbands; and he whom thou now hast is not thy husband: in that saidst thou truly."

I am amazed, and my mouth hangs open like the slow boy who lives up the road from me.  How could this Rabbi know of my past?  No Samaritan would have spoken to him, so how could he have learned of me?  There is no way.

I search his eyes for condemnation, for surely I shall see it, even if through kindness he should try to hide it.  I, who have been put aside five times by the men who claimed to love me and who now live with a man not my husband, have seen condemnation in many eyes over many years. I, who did all I knew to be worthy of love yet have been given not just one, but five Bills of Divorcement. I, who have suffered so from the whims and anger of men. This Rabbi knows all this of me and shall surely now send me away.

Yet even more incredible than this man's discernment is the condemnation I do *not* see in his face. Even though he knows I have had five husbands, I see no question in his eyes as to what fault in me caused them all to divorce me. He knows I am living with a man who is not my husband, but he does not look at me with contempt.

Does he accept me as I am? At this knowledge, something deep within me shifts, as if all the hurts, all the misconceptions, all the mistakes are loosed from my soul, and for a second I catch a glimpse of myself through this man's eyes. Totally different from the picture I have of myself, I see I am more worthy, more deserving of love, even more pure than I ever imagined.

"Sir," I whisper in my amazement, "I perceive that thou art a prophet." I have worshipped the same God as the Jews all my life, and surely there is a purpose that He tells this Rabbi of my shame. "Our fathers worshipped in this mountain," I point to Mount Gerizim where Manasseh built our Samaritan temple, "and ye say, that in Jerusalem is the place where men ought to worship."

"Woman, believe me," the man addresses me in the ordinary manner of a man honorably addressing a woman, "the hour cometh when ye shall neither in this mountain, nor yet at Jerusalem, worship the Father. Ye worship ye know not what: we know what we worship: for salvation is of the Jews. But the hour cometh, and now is, when the true worshippers shall worship the Father in spirit and in truth: for the Father seekest such to worship him. God is a spirit: and they that worship him must worship him in spirit and in truth."

Could it be that this Rabbi is saying the Father seekest those such as I? No, it cannot be, for why would the Father want one so unworthy to worship at His feet?

As we speak, other men, also Jews, join us at the well. They are obviously with the prophet, and I can tell by their expressions that they marvel. I wonder if they marvel more that he speaks with a woman, or a Samaritan.

Yet they marvel no more than I. I have never had a man speak with me thus, engage me in a conversation where I had to strain to understand the meaning of the words or speak to me as though I were His equal.

I want these men to know that this honor is not given me in vain, that I have been well taught by my father, well enough to know what I worship. "I know the Messiah cometh, which is called Christ," I say. "When He is come, He will tell us all things."

This prophet leans forward, and his eyes shine with that light again. When he speaks, though his words are quiet, they strike to my very soul. *"I that speak unto thee am he."*

The Messiah? Can it be? I have marveled that any man would speak to me thus, but the Messiah? Why would He speak to one such as I?

I am confused. Amazed. Stunned. Yet did He not tell me all things which I had done?

As I gaze into His eyes, they burn with an intensity I have never before felt, but an intensity of peace and of love that refreshes my soul. I could look into His eyes forever and feel this love.

I knew He was a prophet, but now I see in His eyes that He does speak the truth. This man *is* the Messiah. The Christ has revealed his identity to me. To *me*, who has never felt worthy of the love of man.

The Messiah offers me love without question, acceptance without condemnation, understanding without ridicule. For the first time in my life, I do not care about the thoughts of others, for the Messiah loves me.

I fall to my knees before Him to worship. Now I understand that He has not been speaking of water to replace that from the well, but that this living water is for my soul for I feel as a parched plant which has received life-giving water. I feel the need to share it with others, to let them drink of the living water also.

I stand, leave my water pot, and run into the city. Strangely, I am no longer afraid to talk with people. I am not afraid of what they think of me, for I am filled with peace, with a sense of self-worth.

As I run through the streets, people even look at me differently. The women do not look away, and the men look into my *eyes*.

I call out to all of them, men and women alike, crying, "Come, see a man, which told me all things that ever I did: is not this the Christ?" I continue to run through the city, crying out these words, to announce the Christ who first revealed Himself to me.

I hurry to find Rashidi. When I do, I run into his arms.

"What is wrong?" he asks in concern.

I laugh with my joy. "There is nothing wrong. The Messiah has spoken with me, and offers living water to all those who will drink." I hold my breath and wait for his reaction to my words. *Please let him believe.*

"The Messiah?" Rashidi asks, but his face softens. "Take me to him."

Relief fills me and I grab his hand. Soon I have spoken to many other Samaritans who also believe my words. They follow me back to the well to find the Christ. Together we beseech Him to tarry with us and teach us, and he agrees to stay two days.

For those two days Rashidi and I drink of the living water. As Christ speaks, my heart is filled with understanding such as I never have known and my cup of joy is full. I stand among the women of my village, sure of God's love for me, no longer shamed. I speak as

I have not dared speak in years, certain of my Lord's understanding.

Many people come to me and tell me, "Now we believe, not because of thy saying: for we have heard Him ourselves, and know that this is indeed the Christ, the Savior of the World."

Yes, He is the Savior of the World. The Christ. He is my Savior, as well. For He has shown me that God seest not as man seest, that my Lord lovest not as man lovest. God does not cease to love one who is imperfect, such as I, nor turn away from one who errs. It was I who turned from God in shame.

I am still amazed. The Messiah spoke with me, a Samaritan. A Samaritan *woman*. A woman five times rejected. A woman now living with a man without a contract of marriage.

Yet Christ did not condemn me, but spoke with me and entrusted me with His message. He spoke to me as a woman worthy of love and respect. He has filled me with respect and love for myself as a daughter of God.

And I see in Rashidi's eyes and hear in his words that he sees himself as more worthy than he ever has. I feel the fullness of his noble spirit and see the light of Christ in his eyes. Though I have loved him greatly before, now I also trust in his love for me. Now when he speaks to me again of a marriage contract, I am no longer afraid.

Because of the miraculous change in me, the people of my village continue to speak to me differently.

I have partaken of the living water the Messiah offers, and my soul has been refreshed with the love of God and the peace of the Messiah. I can begin my life again. I will thirst no more for love, for I have found unconditional love from my Lord.

Blessed be His name forever.

"...Young man,
I say unto thee,
Arise."

*(Luke 7:14)*

# ARISE!

## *Widow Whose Son is Raised from the Dead*

I have cried for the past twelve hours since the other men carried my son's body home after his horrible fall from the rocks. My throat burns from the cries of my mourning, my eyes sting from the ashes I wear, and my knees ache from kneeling by the bier on which his body lies.

My friends and neighbors are here to mourn with me, and the professional woman mourner raises her voice high. But I am exhausted physically and emotionally, numb inside except for the regret that fills me when I realize I did not tell Lateef I loved him for many weeks before he died. I was not angry with him, it was only that I was so caught up in the business of living, the everyday tasks, that I forgot to tell him how important he was to me. Lateef--my gentle son. My only child.

I have washed his body, as I did when he was but a babe. I have rubbed oil into his skin as I cried. Now I take a fragrant mixture of myrrh and aloes, apply it to his skin, and bind it there with the burial clothes. I wrap each long strip of linen around my son's body until only his head remains uncovered. His beautiful face. His strong chin and firm brow. His gentle eyes, now closed forever. A voice inside cries denial. It cannot be

41

so. He is but asleep. See? He cannot be dead. But no breath lifts his narrow chest or leaves his lips. I try to pretend I am only dressing my son, but the truth tears my heart.

It is time to bind his head with a linen napkin, but I pause. I cannot bring myself to cover his face. Not yet.

I am now unclean, for I have touched my son's dead body. I will remain so for seven days, as will my home. But I do not care for that. Lateef is gone. My dear young son, barely past childhood himself, who has cared for me since my husband died. And now I am alone.

More tears sting my eyes and I am surprised to find I have any left to shed. I thought I had already used them all.

"It is time." My good friend Yahra steps beside me, speaking softly. "Do you want me to bind his head for you?"

"No!" I cry out. I cannot have another do this task. This is the last service I can do for my son, and I will make sure it is done right. I force my voice to a more reasonable tone, for she has offered to become unclean herself because of her love for me. "No. I will do it. Only leave me for a moment."

Yahra nods in understanding, and steps back.

I lay my hand against Lateef's forehead. My suckling babe, my unsteady toddler, my energetic youth, my handsome young man, my honorable loving son. How can I go on without you? You have been my only reason for living these past three years since your father died. Who will care for me now? More importantly, who will I care for? For whom will I fix meals? Whose stories will make me laugh? No one. *No one.*

I shall be alone. Even if I pretend all day that you are only gone from home, each evening all pretense will disappear and I will have only pain and loneliness as my companions.

"Oh, Lateef," I whisper. "How can I bear your loss?"

I kiss his forehead, and lightly touch his cheek. The chill of his skin makes me want to cover him with a blanket. But I cannot warm him. It is time--my friend spoke truly. By covering his face I can no longer pretend I am simply dressing him. Yes, it is time, but how can I find the strength I need to face this horrible task? I know only one way.

I draw in a deep breath and close my eyes. Please, God, give me the strength I need, for I know not how to go on without Lateef. Give me strength to bear the pain of his loss.

One more deep breath, and I open my eyes. Then I gently lift Lateef's head and slip the napkin underneath. I caress more of the spiced oil onto his cheeks. Onto his chin, barely beginning to grow wisps of a beard. His neck. His forehead. Then I can do no more. I cannot put off this horrible moment any longer. I tie the napkin over his face.

Now that I see him as a body ready for burial, I rend my sackcloth tunic--this horrible goat-hair garment I wear for mourning. I throw myself over the bundle of linen clothes that used to be my son, yet is now only his body, and raise my voice to the heavens.

That is the signal to the others. They lift me to my feet, as the four men who have agreed to carry my son's bier each take a corner pole and lift it up. And thus my son leads a funeral procession. This young vibrant youth who honored his mother and the law and his God. It was hard enough to bury his father, but I always imagined Lateef would bury me.

*Why, God? Why did you take my son and leave me behind?* This is not the order of things. I do not understand. My tears begin anew, and they are as blood flowing from my breaking heart.

If only I had not spoken so sharply to him yesterday. And over what? Some inconsequential thing. I whisper, "I am sorry, Lateef," but for what good? He cannot hear me. "I love you," I say, but he does not hear this either. It is too late for such words.

I take my place beside the bier. Before nightfall, Lateef will rest on a ledge in a cave, his bed a cold, silent grave with a boulder rolled before the entrance to keep out the scavengers. And I will be alone with my pain, my grief, my regrets.

It is more than I can stand. Please, God, help me bear this pain. I cannot live with the unfairness of Lateef's death before my own.

The professional mourner leads the crowd in its tumultuous song. A flute player adds to the noise, and each sound clashes against the others. The result sounds as discordant as I feel inside.

As we weave our way through the streets of Nain toward the hillside caves, I lower my head. I do not know how I can do this. But I have no choice. Many people of the city walk beside us, for Lateef was loved by all who knew him, such a good boy, and his father was well respected. The support of my friends gives me the strength I need to bear this pain.

I hear shouts ahead and I look up to see a crowd approaching from the right at the crossroad ahead. Many wave palm fronds and cry out, "Hosanna." I know of no wedding in Nain today, and I see no bride. But at the head of the crowd is a handful of men I do not know, and there is one who looks as if he could be the bridegroom, yet he carries a small child in his arms. At least he seems to be the one the crowd follows. As we approach, he motions to the others to stop and he watches me closely, as if he has seen many widows mourning the loss of their only son. A look of compassion fills his face, and I feel his concern even from this distance. Fresh tears come to my eyes. His sorrow touches me, though I do not understand why he should care about a stranger's grief.

When we reach the crowd, the leader gently places the child on the ground and pats his head, then he steps in front of me and halts my progress. Such kindness fills his eyes that my heart seems to relax and my tears to slow. "Weep not," he says to me, and the words carry a surprising comfort which somehow calms my wounded soul. He touches the bier, and they that bear my son stand still.

What is the power of this man that he can enter into a funeral procession and none will stop him? He will be unclean if he touches Lateef's body--does he not know this? I should warn him, but I cannot find the strength to speak.

As he looks at the linen-clad body of my son, the crowd of mourners and this man's followers fall silent. The quiet is sudden and disquieting. He motions for the bearers to place the bier on the ground. Fear grows within me, for I know not what he will do with my son.

As if he senses my turmoil, he turns back toward me. Looking into his eyes, I know no fear. This man means no harm to Lateef. But who is he? And what is he doing?

He kneels beside the bier and says, in a voice pulsing with power, "Young man, I say unto thee, *Arise.*"

Does this man not understand what is happening? My neighbors mutter my silent questions aloud: Who is this man? Is he demented?

But I hear one of his followers cry out, "Watch. Jesus performs another miracle."

Of a sudden, my son's body seems to move. It cannot be. It must be a trick of the light. Or a spell. Is it possible that I could be under this man's spell so quickly?

But there--Lateef sits up. I gasp in awe and people around me jump with fear. Some even scream. The women around me scatter. Even my friend Yahra runs to the far side of the road and hides behind an olive tree. My legs grow so weak that I drop to the ground and sit, held in place by my own fear. I do not faint, though I feel light-headed. My son is *dead*. He still wears the linen funeral clothes, even over his face. I *know* he is dead. I prepared his body for burial myself. I kissed his cold and lifeless forehead.

He is *dead*!

Yet he obeys this man's command and sits. What manner of man can command even the dead? I am numb with shock.

This man kneels beside Lateef, unties the linen napkin, and gently uses the napkin to wipe the spices from my son's face. My son blinks in the sun's light, but how can this be? How can this man have the power to change death into life? Only *God* Himself could command that.

Is he God? Or God's prophet? He must be one or the other for this deed is surely done only through God's power.

With the spiced oil still shimmering on the skin of his face, Lateef looks at me. "Mother," is his first word uttered, as it was when he was a babe.

The word brings me from my shock and I cry out in joy, "My son!" *My son is alive!* I know not how, only that a miracle has brought him back to me. One of this

47

man's believers helps me rise from the ground, but my legs are still weak.

I long to rush to my son, but I wait, trembling, as this man of God unwraps the linen strips from my son's body, helps him to his feet, and covers him with his own robe. He walks Lateef to me and puts his hand in mine. "Here is your son, good woman."

I open my arms and embrace my son. Tears of joy replace those of anguish. I cannot begin to describe my joy in that moment as I kiss Lateef's hands and cry and laugh all at the same time. Wasting no time, I say the words I had left unsaid before. "I love you, my son."

Lateef wraps his arms around me and holds me as I weep with joy. Finally, I lift my head from his shoulder, and look at this stranger who performs godly miracles. "Thank you," I say, but the words are inadequate and my voice barely sounds above a whisper. "Praise God."

This man acknowledges my words with a nod and a gentle smile, and in his eyes I see all the love of the ages.

I must know who has given my son back to me, who it is that wields the powers of God to command the very dead to rise, and so I ask him, "Who art thou?"

"I am," he replies, "Jesus of Nazareth."

At his words, yet another miracle occurs and I see my beloved husband standing by my side. And I know in that moment he has been at my side throughout my ordeal. Now he speaks with the same familiar voice I remember so well. "This is Jesus the Christ, Our Savior, The Messiah, the Son of God. Know you now who to thank." My husband motions toward Jesus of Nazareth, and then is gone again.

Lateef wraps his still-weak arm more tightly around me to try to support me as I look back at Jesus with awe and trembling.

I look into the eyes of the Messiah and feel a love that fills my world, and I have the answer to my question. "Thank you," I repeat, and begin to say more, but the Son of God motions for silence.

"Take your son home, good mother," He says gently. "He has need of rest." Without waiting, He rejoins his disciples and lifts the child again. He continues on His way, followed by the large crowd again singing Hosannas.

"Hosanna," I echo. Hosanna to God in the highest. Hosanna to the Son of God here among us. Hosanna to Immanuel, for God is With Us. Hosanna.

All around me, my neighbors and friends stand with fear in their eyes. One lifts her voice in song and glorifies God, saying that a great prophet is risen up among us. Another says that God hath visited his people.

They are right. God walks among us, performing mighty, wonderful miracles. I prayed to God and He returned my son to me. His Son raised mine from the dead. And why? Because He loves me and so felt compassion for me. He returned Lateef to me. He allowed me to see my beloved husband and to know he is at peace. Truly I am no longer alone, and never have been. He allowed me to know my husband lives still, in another place, and that he waits for me.

Glory to God, who loves His children with a perfect love. Praise Him who felt compassion for a widow who lost her only son. Honor Him who would bestow such a gift.

I marvel that it was my son raised from the dead. I am certain Jesus raised my son for a purpose, but He told me not why. Surely there are other women who have lost husbands, other mothers whose children have gone before, other women whose grief this Jesus has seen.

As I ponder, I understand. These feelings slowly begin to burn within my bosom. This knowledge cries to be spread abroad. God has raised my son, and now I must testify to others what I have learned.

I will thank the Lord my God by sharing this miraculous gift of life after death with others who grieve. I shall console them with this wondrous promise. I shall help them to know the separation of death is only temporary. For as God has raised my son today, so shall He raise us all and give us life everlasting.

Abandoning the bier in the street, I walk back to my home with my arms around my son, my heart full of gratitude. Again I cry, but these are tears of joy and not of grief. I keep my arms wrapped tightly around my son. I dare not let him go, for he is too newly returned to me.

Never again shall I allow my daily troubles make me forget what is truly important. Never again shall I take for granted that I shall have time to show my love at a later hour. Never again shall I forget that most precious gift, the gift of life even after death.

Thank you, God. Thank you for my son and for Thine. For the gift of life eternal. For another chance to tell Lateef of my love for him.

"...and began to wash
his feet with tears,
and did wipe them
with the hairs
of her head..."

*(Luke 7:38)*

# WASHED CLEAN

## *Woman Who Washes Christ's Feet With Her Tears*

I am a sinner, a weak and wretched thing. My sins have long haunted me, but never before as they have for these past few days since I heard Jesus speak. I have not even left my home as I remember first one sin, then another, and still another. I shudder with revulsion at each in turn. I have forsaken my sins long ago, but they are not forgotten. And I know there is nothing I can do to remove the stain of them from upon my soul.

How could I have committed such vile acts? I could not do so now, but I did, and by so doing have brought sorrow, humiliation, and damnation upon myself.

I would not force any to suffer the hearing of my sins. But I suffer the remembering as my mind goes from one to the next--reliving another moment of weakness--cringing on the floor as yet another wave of self-loathing washes over me.

I am the lowest of all people. I cannot bear to live as I once did, but what am I to do now? There is no way to retrieve the innocence of childhood or the promise of youth. In my weakness, I threw it all away. Now I live each day with the pains of the damned--for that I am. I cannot hope to have my gruesome sins forgiven. They are too numerous, too serious, too painful to remember. Yet still they flood my mind.

I cry out to the Lord in prayer, asking for His help, though I would not wonder if he refrained from listening to one such as I, if He does not shudder in revulsion at the mere thought of me. His laws were known to me, even as I disobeyed them.

Someone knocks upon my door. I do not answer it, but nevertheless it opens. Not wanting any to find me in such a state, I sit up quickly. When Mareshah enters, I try to hide my tears of pain from her.

"My friend," she cries as she sees me on the floor. She kneels beside me and places an arm around my shoulders. "Are you yet suffering?"

"Not so much now," I lie, and try to hide my pain. But we have been friends far too long to pretend. She hears the lie as it leaves my lips. She reaches out and tucks in a lock of my hair which has fallen out of place. "You are still suffering."

"Yes," I admit, and brush a tear from my cheek.

"But Jesus spoke of hope. *I am the Way*--Is that not what He said?"

I shake my head. "While I listened to His words I felt hope for forgiveness, when I was baptized I was sure of it, but here in my home my sins wipe away any hope. I have forsaken my right to forgiveness."

My friend's eyes shine brightly with her caring. "You did not understand what He said. You need to hear Him speak again. You can, for He is here in Nain, and will soon be sitting at meat in the house of Simon the Pharisee. Go see Him."

"Jesus is here?" I ask, and my voice is faint in my own ears.

"That is what I have come to tell you. Since we traveled to hear Him speak, He has performed many marvelous miracles. He healed a Centurion's servant with just a word right outside of Nain, and the next day he raised a widow's son from the dead as he lay on the bier. From the very dead! And if you had not been as the dead yourself, hidden away in the dark of your house, you would have heard, as has everyone in Nain with ears to hear. Oh, yes, my dear friend, as long as there is a Savior, there is hope."

My excitement rises, only to die again. Surely this widow whose son has been raised from the dead is a virtuous woman, whereas I can claim no such past. Perhaps a virtuous woman would not feel the same frantic need I do to see Jesus, and to give Him homage. But the pain of my sins makes me desperate to regain the hope of forgiveness I had before in His presence. A nagging voice inside me warns that He will not want a sinner there. I pause. He did not send me away before but then I stood in the midst of a crowd. If He cannot stand the sight of me this evening, He has only to send me away and I will go. But I hope He does not. I pray He does not.

My friend helps me to my feet and hugs me, then leaves as quickly as she came, to go to her mother's house with the news.

Of a sudden, the beautiful, finely crafted alabaster box filled with expensive ointment on my shelf catches my eye. When I purchased it, I spent far more than I could afford, not knowing for what purpose I would use it. Now I know.

Reaching high to retrieve the box, I clutch it to my bosom. Rushing toward the house of Simon, the Pharisee, I try to gather enough courage to carry out my plan. I will go inside and anoint Jesus' feet with my ointment, listen to Him speak to regain my hope, then leave again without disturbing anyone. I try to turn my thoughts from fear to hope lest I lose the last of my courage.

I pause at the entrance to Simon's house. I am not the only visitor to enter seeking Jesus this night. But I am the lowest sinner here. And I see by the looks from others that they also recognize this fact. Simon will doubtless disapprove of my disturbing one of his guests. He might even remove me from his home. But I do not care--my pain is too great and I seek the peace I found before in Jesus' presence.

As I enter, I see Jesus has not yet arrived. I wait for him, still clutching the alabaster box to my bosom as if I am afraid someone might snatch it. Hardly breathing because of my great anxiety and excitement, I wait.

Soon after I arrive, a crowd begins to gather. The men have arrived. Jesus enters the room followed by the disciples I saw with Him the other day. Simon greets them and bids them sit.

But Simon does no honor to Jesus and His men for he has no one wash the dust from their feet and their hands. Without comment, Jesus reclines on His side on one of the couches surrounding the table, and leans on one elbow to eat. I feel His presence even from where I stand. As before when I stood in the crowd and listened, I feel His divinity and His majesty.

I circle the outer rim of the room, weaving between women bearing serving plates for the men at the table, and other visitors such as myself along the walls. No one pays attention to the women, so I am not noticed.

All the while I watch Jesus, and awe fills my soul. I feel hope rekindle within me just being in the same room with Him.

As if Jesus senses a sinner, he looks up. His eyes meet mine.

I stop as a wave of love sweeps through me such as I have never felt before, and this love brushes aside the painful web of my sins. The spirit bears witness to my soul in this moment of who this Jesus is. He is the Christ, the Son of God, the promised Messiah, and as such can see clear to the center of my very soul and read the depths thereof. He sees my terrible sins--the ones which cause me to suffer so--but he does *not* shudder in revulsion. I see my sins do not matter as a way to judge me, but He is sad for the hurt I have brought upon myself.

I cannot hold back my tears. He loves me! And His love melts away my pain. I am filled with joy, and hope burns bright within my bosom. Hope that I can be forgiven some day.

Simon says something so softly I cannot hear. Christ looks back at him and responds. And I am left shaken from the power of just a look into His eyes. It is several moments before I find the strength to move again.

When I do, I search the faces of the others in the room. They do not appear shaken to their very souls as I am, not even those who are here to see Jesus. Do they not realize who He really is? Do they not feel the power of His very presence? How could they not? But I can tell by looking at them that they do not. Why are they here then? Words of his deeds precede Him and perhaps for this reason alone they follow Him. *Yet they do not realize who He is.*

I continue to circle the room until I am behind the couch upon which Christ rests. I kneel at the end of the couch and my tears flow heavily down my cheeks, as though my shame fell liquid from my eyes.

The spirit of Christ fills the air around Him. It encircles me with a love so sweet and strong that it seems to pull the tears from my eyes. I begin to sob and my tears gush forth. I cannot stop. As I lean over, my tears drip from my cheeks onto His feet--the feet of my Lord.

The tears streak through the dust there. I weep great tears as I--a sinner--worship my Lord. I cry from shame of my sins, deep regret and a desire for blessed forgiveness.

And I cry because none have acknowledged the greatness of this man or even done Him this simple service. I cannot believe no one has bothered to wash His feet. No honor has been done Him. So I, who am unworthy to be in His presence, wash His feet clean of the road's dust with my tears.

While I minister to my Lord, the men continue to talk among themselves and they do not notice me. I have nothing with which to dry His feet, so I pull the pin from my hair. It falls loose down my back. I lean to take a handful of my hair and use it to wipe my Master's feet dry, caressing and wiping, caressing and wiping.

When they are dry, I kiss one foot, and then the other. My Lord. My Master.

Now I lift the lid of my alabaster box, reach in and anoint my Lord's feet with the ointment. Even this expensive ointment seems inadequate in His presence, but it is the best I have to offer.

I sit up, looking straight into the eyes of Simon, the Pharisee. He flicks his eyes away and a look of contempt flashes across his rigid features. There is no doubt what he thinks of me--he would not suffer one such as I to touch *him*. I fear he will send me away. But I could not bear to leave Christ's presence--not yet.

Jesus seems to notice the flash of contempt on Simon's face, for He says, "Simon, I have somewhat to say unto thee." His very voice calms my soul and soothes my pain.

Simon smiles as one who would please another. "Master, say on."

I gently massage ointment into the ball of the foot, that part which wearies most with walking, and listen as Christ speaks. "There was a certain creditor which had two debtors: the one owed five hundred pence, and the other fifty. And when they had nothing to pay, he frankly forgave them both. Tell me therefore, which of them will love him most?"

Simon pauses with a fig in his hand ready to place in his mouth. "I suppose that he to whom he forgave most."

Jesus said, "Thou has rightly judged." When He turns and pushes to a sitting position on the couch, I raise my gaze to Him. Our eyes connect again and His love washes through me as before. All thoughts leave my mind as I look into the eyes of my Savior, and find hope of salvation there. "Seest thou this woman? I entered into thy house, thou gavest me no water for my feet: but she hath washed my feet with tears, and wiped them with the hairs of her head."

No other man here would acknowledge service from a woman. It is expected that a woman serve a man. I listen with amazement as Christ acknowledges my simple service, and my soul fills with joy at His words.

Jesus looks back at Simon and motions in my direction. "Thou gavest me no kiss: but this woman since the time I came in hath not ceased to kiss my feet."

I listen and grow uncomfortable with the attention of all upon me. Afraid Simon might decide to cast me from his house, I twist my hair back into place and replace the pin to hold it.

Jesus speaks on. "My head with oil thou didst not anoint: but this woman hath anointeth my feet with ointment. Wherefore I say unto thee, her sins, which are many, are forgiven; for she loved much: but to whom little is forgiven, the same loveth little."

Yes, my sins are many. But their power to haunt me fades even as He speaks the words. *My sins are forgiven!* My heart sings with joy at the realization.

Christ looks at me again, and in His eyes is such love it overflows the boundaries of my soul until I am totally consumed with it--a love so strong, I feel it in my entire being. It quickens my heart and pulses with my blood. It warms me and sets my being on fire as the air is charged during a storm.

Ignoring the others, Christ speaks directly to me. His voice softens as He says, "*Thy sins are forgiven.*"

Tears overflow my eyes again. Tears of joy. *I am forgiven of my horrible sins!*

Then He turns back to Simon as if to check Simon's reaction to His words. Only when He takes His eyes from mine do I notice the other people at the table who sit at meat, and I can tell by their expressions that they wonder who this is that forgiveth sins also. I am sorry that they are unable to feel what I feel, to know what I know.

What they think of me now matters not. They eat at meat with Christ, but they do not understand who He is. My Lord--the Messiah Himself--hath forgiven my sins. I am clean every whit. The vile sins which have haunted me are gone forever, replaced by joy. He has saved my wicked soul.

Christ turns and once more gazes into my eyes. "Thy faith hath saved thee," He says gently. "Go in peace."

My joy is complete for my Lord has forgiven me. Now I can forgive myself.

For the first time in many, many years, my soul is at peace.

"...Daughter,
be of good comfort,
Thy faith hath made
thee whole..."

*(Matthew 9:22)*

# THE HEALING TOUCH
## *Woman Who Touches Christ's Hem and is Healed*

I hear excited voices just outside the gate in the wall encircling the courtyard of my home. Usually people do not come so close to the gate of one unclean, but in their excitement they must not notice where they stand.

It is seldom I am close enough to others to hear their conversation. Walking quietly along the inside of the wall so I may not be seen, I hide behind the grapevine which grows there. I creep closer until I can make out their words.

"He is on his way to heal the daughter of Jairus," one woman says. "I heard Jairus ask, and he follows Jairus now to his home."

Another woman's voice rises shrill above the wall. "They say he has healed many--the blind, the lame, the lepers."

A healer? For an instant hope fills me, then just as quickly dies again. I know this Jairus--he is one of the rulers of the synagogue--so I am not surprised that this healer answers his request. But if one such as I--without import, without wealth--were to ask, would this healer so readily agree?

"Ha!" A third woman makes a derisive sound. "I do not believe anyone can heal in that manner. I say he is a fraud."

Yet a fourth woman speaks, and her voice is so quiet I have to strain to hear her words. "I have heard of this Jesus of Nazareth. Some say He is the Son of God."

Jesus of Nazareth? My hope returns. I, too, have heard much of him. I, too, have heard the stories of people he has healed. I know not whether he is the Son of God, but my heart sings with a hope which I thought was gone forever. The hope which always before cost me so much and then was shattered into pieces.

For the past twelve years, I have been plagued by an issue of blood. I have been visited by many physicians during these years, suffered many things of each of them, and spent all that I had. They took my money until there was no more, but none healed me. Rather I have grown worse. And on this day I am still unclean.

But if I go to *this* healer, perhaps I can be made whole again. He is a healer, a physician--perhaps even the Son of God. I would lose nothing by going, yet I have everything to gain.

Still I hesitate, for I am unclean and am forbidden to go among others. Even the very chairs I sit in and bed I sleep upon are unclean. Any person who touches me would then be required to return home to bathe their bodies and wash their clothes and they would themselves be unclean until the even. Oh, that I could be made clean by simply washing and sleeping! Scrub though I may, every day when I rise I am still unclean.

I sense this Jesus of Nazareth can make me whole. But I will need to cover my face so none will know me and I can slip through the crowd undetected. None need know why I have come. And after seven days I could do what I have dreamed of for twelve long years--I could take the two animals required to the temple, one for the burnt offering and one for the sin sacrifice, and then the priest would declare me clean. I can no longer afford a lamb with the pigeon, so I would take two pigeons. I sigh at the hope of becoming clean. For twelve years I have hoped in vain. Twelve years have I suffered this curse. *Twelve years.* Long enough for a babe to grow nigh to manhood, for a girl child to become a woman, more than enough time for an olive tree seedling to mature and bear fruit.

Long enough. My resolve strengthens. I am a fool to hesitate while this healer walks the streets of my city. I will go.

I creep back along the wall the way I came, and then run into my home to find my mantle. I wrap it around my head, and then tuck it in so it veils and shadows my face. Slowly, I step out my door and onto the street. My breath catches when I realize the women still stand there but, intent in their conversation, they do not notice me. I slip to the corner, and then run to the place where I think the procession will be by this time.

When I have run so far I must stop to catch my breath, I see a crowd coming up behind me. Seeing the large number of people around him, I begin to doubt that I can draw the attention of Jesus. If he is truly a healer, perhaps I can just touch him in the crowd and that will be enough.

My first sight of Jesus of Nazareth stuns me. I need no one to tell me which man is he--no one could mistake his presence. He closes the distance between us quickly with his long strides. I can see his seamless robe and it tells me je is a teacher and a preacher. The border of his robe identifies him as the physician and healer I have heard him described. But the story his robes tell are nothing compared to his face.

He has the look of a leader, strong and handsome, and he strides confidently through the crowd which follows him as people hungry for a meal only he can provide.

But the most astonishing thing about him is that he seems to glow. Even here, in the sunlight, I see an aura of light surrounding his being. His head is haloed and even his clothes give off this light.

A man walks on the road across from me, also watching Jesus. I glance to see his reaction to this radiant man, but I see no awe in his face such as fills my heart. Can it be possible that he does not see the light? How can he not? Is he like that woman at my gate who did not believe?

Yet I cannot keep my eyes from Jesus of Nazareth. Surely He *is* the Son of God, and surely He *can* heal me. And even as I know this, I also know I cannot touch this magnificent being and thus make Him unclean. Still a peace fills me--if I touch only His robe, even that will heal me.

I have had false hopes many times over the past twelve years, but what I feel now is a certainty, a serenity. If I can only touch Him today, I will not have this issue of blood tomorrow. I have to reach Jesus.

The crowd draws near, and I can recognize clearly on the faces of the crowd the few people who see the light and the many others who do not.

I lean against the wall until He passes, then I take a step to the back of the crowd that walks behind Him. But a habit of twelve years is difficult to overcome. I am suddenly surrounded by people and I panic. I cannot move to the right or the left without touching someone and making them unclean. I cannot move ahead without touching two people.

A new fear arises within me. What will happen if these people discover who I am? What will they do to me for going among them when I knew I must not? For making them unclean?

I try to act as though I belong here, for I do not want to give myself away. I force my mind back, to remember how it felt to be clean and walk among a crowd, This many people makes my head dizzy. *It has been so long.*

I swallow my fear. Jesus is farther from me now, and I must reach Him. If I cannot keep from touching others then that is what I must do. I take a deep breath, run to catch up, and I cannot avoid brushing against people. In my mind, I utter apologies to them, but aloud I say nothing. I try not to push against a woman carrying a child, but I do. I touch an old man. A young man in expensive robes. In their eagerness to be close to Jesus, the crowd blocks my path. But I *must* reach him. I must. I adjust my mantle so it is pulled tight across my face, and I jostle into place closer and closer to Jesus.

Through the throng of people I can see Jesus and His apostles, but try as I might I cannot reach them. I catch glimpses of His robe. If I cannot reach Him, perhaps I can just touch His sleeve, and then slip away without any knowing what I have done. But first I must reach His sleeve.

I push between a man and an old woman, and I cringe. But I am one step closer to this healer, one step closer to being clean, almost within reach of Him now.

An opening appears before me, and I lunge for it, but the crowd shifts and cuts me off. Now I am directly behind Christ, but many people are still between us. I cannot reach Him! But I must! *I must!*

As Jesus walks, the hem of His robe flutters with His movement. The healer's border. If I cannot reach Jesus Himself, or even the sleeve of His robe, still if I but touch the border of His garment, I know I will be healed. As I am pushed back, desperation fills me. We are almost to the home of Jairus now, and Jesus will go inside. I must touch His robe *now!*

I gather my strength and push through. There--the hem is before me, within my grasp. Quickly I reach out and touch the glowing border.

Instantly warm, loving, healing energy flows through my fingers, my hand, my arm, to my very center. Straightway I feel the fountain of my blood is dried. In awe, scarcely able to breathe, I release the hem. I can feel within myself that I am healed of my plague, and the wonder of it stays my steps. I prayed to God to heal me and He sent His very Son in answer.

The crowd moves on without me. Yet before Christ goes two more steps and before I can slip away, He turns and asks, "Who touched me?"

He does not sound angry, only curious, but fear clenches my throat. People around me deny having touched Him. I dare not speak.

"Master, the multitude throng thee and press thee," one of His apostles says incredulously, "and sayest thou, Who touchest me?"

"Somebody hath touched me," Christ insists and looks around the crowd, "for I perceive that virtue is gone out of me."

I know some of His healing energy left Him and entered me for I felt it as it healed me, and this is that virtue of which He speaks. Do I glow with His energy and thus give myself away? Quickly I look, but I see no glow upon my hands.

A fresh fear arises. When I took His healing energy without asking, did I steal it? Will He take it back? Can I go back to my sickness after being whole even for a moment? Or will He punish me for stealing? Will he ask this crowd to punish me?

I hold my breath as I wait. Surely He cannot tell it was I. But He is *The Christ*. He must be. The Son of God. Surely He *will* know. I release the air from my lungs, but I must force my body to take in the very air it needs, for my fear paralyzes me.

Jesus looks around slowly, scanning the crowd.

When He looks into my eyes, He pauses, as if He knows. Of course He knows. The Son of God looks into my face and He knows I have stolen His healing energy. His face holds no anger, only glows with love, but my guilt dries my tongue and sets my body to trembling with fear. I cannot lie to the Son of God. As I stumble forward toward Christ, the crowd pushes back from me. I fall down before Him, and the dust from the road rises into my nostrils, choking me.

"It was I who touched Thee, Lord. I have had an issue of blood for these past twelve years." As I confess, I hear the crowd recoil as they realize I might have touched them and made them unclean. I rush to explain to them all why I had done so, to explain to Him. "And I knew if I could only touch Thy clothes I would be healed." My voice chokes with emotion and

I begin to cry. "And I can feel within myself that I am healed."

"Daughter, be of good comfort," Jesus says. He touches my arm, as if I have never been unclean, and helps me to my feet, and wipes a tear from my cheek. His eyes are filled with love--that same love which surrounds Him and with which He glows. "Thy faith hath made thee whole."

I cannot still my trembling, but I manage to stand on my unsteady feet.

"Go in peace." He says and my entire frame is filled with the love, the light. His eyes catch mine, and I cannot pull my gaze away from the love I find there. He smiles gently. "And be whole of thy plague."

He will let me stay whole! Joy fills me at the goodness of my Lord and more tears flow down my cheeks, but these are of pure happiness and gratitude.

While Christ yet speaks thus to me, another man comes and says to Jairus, "Thy daughter is dead; trouble not the Master."

Jesus turns from me then. He looks at Jairus and declares in a voice filled with power, "Fear not: believe only, and she shall be made whole."

Once again He strides toward the home of Jairus, and the crowd follows Him as before. But I remain standing behind, still unsteady on my feet. Wonder fills me at the miracle of it.

His words play through my mind: *Thy faith hath made thee whole.* I can scarce take it in. Without *my*

73

faith, could not the miracle have been performed? The warmth in my bosom tells me this is so. Had I but doubted Christ, even for a moment, I would be unclean still.

Tears of wonder fill my eyes. I fall once again to my knees and thank the Lord my God for this miracle, for sending His Son to come among us to work His miracles.

I am healed. I touched Christ's hem and I am healed.

So will be the daughter of Jairus.

So will be all who believe.

"For a certain woman,
whose young daughter
had an unclean spirit,
heard of Him,
and came
and fell at His feet."

*(Mark 7:25)*

# CRUMBS FROM THE
# MASTER'S TABLE
## *Gentile Woman*
## *Whose Daughter is Healed*

I have come a great distance to find the one they call Jesus. I am not from Israel nor am I a Jew. Rather I am a Greek, a Syrophenician by nation. But I have heard of one who can save my daughter, and have followed Him to the borders of Tyre and Sidon. Finally, after days of travel, I have found this Son of David, the heir to the Jewish throne through the great Jewish king. And I have been led to the house which He has entered into.

As I wander into the courtyard, I see five children seated around an outside table. The sight is so normal that it makes me stop. As I watch, my heart aches, for one is a little girl near the age of my Yalena. My sweet Yalena, my youngest, whom I named *Light* for the light she brought into my home and my heart, but she is filled with only darkness now. I watch this child before me eat, and I remember when my Yalena sat at a table. When she could hold a cup. When she did not drool. When she was . . . a normal child.

My little Yalena is ill with a devil. When I look into her eyes, what stares out is not Yalena, but a dark creature. And this dark creature makes Yalena do what she has never done before, not in her five years. She no longer speaks our language or any other, but only gibberish. Her flesh wastes away each day, and I fear this devil will destroy her body along with her spirit if it is not stopped.

I want my daughter back. I want her to sit at table with my other children. To toss down meat to our little dog, just as these children at this table toss down nuggets of food to their two little dogs when their mother is not watching.

I blink back tears. I have been gone long from my home. While I am gone, my dear sister watches over Yalena, and tends to my home and my other children.

I--who have always let other people decide for me, who have let others sway my actions, who have always been afraid to speak for myself--have decided. I will not return until I have spoken with the one they call Jesus, for I have heard He can heal even those who are not present. Thus He can also heal my daughter.

In another corner of the courtyard, I see a chair, and a man seated there. I know in that moment I first see Him that He is Jesus. How do I know? I cannot say, except that I feel His goodness, even from across the courtyard.

In this moment I also know, without a doubt, that this man truly is the Messiah I have heard of. He is the Son of God rumored. He is all I have heard others say He is. And thus truly He can heal my daughter. My heart leaps within me for joy, the first joy I have felt since the darkness entered my daughter.

I cross the courtyard, past the fig tree and the pond of fishes and the children at table. As I draw close to the man, He looks up at me.

I fall at His feet, and cry out, "Have mercy on me, O Lord, thou Son of David; my daughter is grievously vexed with a devil. Please, Lord, I beg Thee, cast forth the devil out of my daughter."

He is silent, and finally I look up into His eyes. I see and feel the great compassion He has for me and my suffering, but He answers me not a word. I beg Him again but He shakes His head in sadness.

Why will He not answer me?

For a second, my courage fails me. Before this day, I would have become discouraged at His refusal to speak and left, but today I cannot. I have come for a purpose and I will do what needs be done. If He will not speak to me now, perhaps that is the custom here, and I will find others to intercede for me.

I rise to my feet and go to find the men who are His disciples, for all great men have disciples, and this man is the greatest of them all. I find one large man whom the others call Peter and I repeat my request to him. He listens with compassion, but says he cannot help me.

Over the next hours, I go from one to the other, begging for them to intercede in behalf of my daughter. One after the other, they tell me they cannot help me.

I can see they grow exasperated with me. Let them. I cannot return to the darkness that used to be my daughter. I will not. Not when there is one who can heal her. And this man Jesus, this Son of David, is that one. He *can* heal Yalena, and so I cannot leave.

When the disciples go into the courtyard, I follow them. I hear them telling Jesus to send me away because I cry after them. I hold my breath as hope grips me. Even as I pray for courage, a faint smile comes to my lips, for a thought of comfort comes to me that, without realizing they are doing so, these disciples have stepped forward to intercede. Not in my behalf, but they have brought me again to their Master's attention. If He turns me away now, I will return tomorrow. And the next day. I have already felt His great love for me. I know He will help me.

"Will you not hear her, Master?" One disciple finally speaks for me, but I wonder if he simply wants me heard so I will leave.

Their Master answers, saying, "I am not sent but unto the lost sheep of the house of Israel."

It is true that I do not belong to the house of Israel, but no mother in Israel could love her daughter more than do I. And my great love for her gives me courage beyond my own, enough to walk into the courtyard again.

I bow down before Jesus and worship Him. "Blessed art Thou, Jesus of Nazareth. Surely Thou art the Son of God. And surely Thou can cast forth the devil from my daughter. Please, Lord, please, save my daughter from the darkness."

I look into His eyes and once again see the love He has for me. Such love I feel that warmth fills my bosom. I know He loves my daughter, as well. But with sadness, He says, "Let the children first be filled, for it is not meet to take the children's bread and to cast it unto the dogs."

I know He speaks of the children of His kingdom, the children of Israel. He speaks for His own house, the house of David.

And I speak for the child of my house, of my heart. "Truth, Lord," I say as I point to the children still seated at the table on the far side of the courtyard. Seeing the little girl again, normal as mine used to be, strengthens my resolve. I may only be as a little dog in the kingdom of Israel, a pet and not a child, yet I know the little dogs are cherished by all in the household, even the master. And even a small crumb of this Master's healing power will be enough to save my Yalena. "Truth, Lord," I repeat, "Yet the dogs under the master's table eat of the children's crumbs." I see the Master nod, and my hopes lift.

"O woman, great is thy faith. Be it unto thee even as thou wilt." Jesus smiles at me and I see in His eyes His joy that I had faith enough that He could heal my daughter. "For this saying go thy way. The devil is gone out of thy daughter."

And I know He speaks the truth. Tears spring to my eyes as I fall at His feet and worship Him anew and thank Him, over and over.

Then I begin my long journey home. During the days and nights of travel, I cherish the memory of His words and His love and His promise.

And when I reach my house, my sister greets me with joy and tells me that the devil has gone out of Yalena, days ago. Indeed, she was made whole from the very hour Jesus spoke.

My daughter is now laid on the bed, sleeping and resting. Once again she is beautiful, whole, normal. When she hears me and opens her eyes, it is my daughter looking out at me through her beautiful light brown eyes. She reaches up her tiny arms and hugs me tight, something she has not done for what seems to have been forever.

I cannot blink back my tears, but they fall freely.

Once again, Yalena stands for light.

Praise be to Jesus, the Son of David, the one with compassion in His eyes, healing in His wings, and light to end all darkness.

"Now Moses in the law
commandeth us,
that such should be stoned:
but what sayest thou?"

*(John 8:5)*

# IN THE VERY ACT
## *Adulteress*

The eldest Pharisee drags me along, gripping my arm so tightly I blink back tears. He sets such a pace that I have to half-run to keep up, while he and the lesser Pharisees stride along swiftly on their long legs. The sun is barely peeking above the Mount of Olives, but before it has completely risen, I will die. I have seen a stoning before, and it is a horribly slow, painful death. I cannot control the trembling in my arms and legs and I stumble again.

The penalty for being with Hamadi is death. I have always known this. Why did I never think I would have to pay the price? Did love blind me to reality? Did I really believe we would not be caught? I begin to pray, then catch myself. How can I pray to my God when I have broken His law? He does not want to hear from a sinner.

I cannot begin to describe the horrible tangle of my feelings when these men burst in upon us--my terror, my shame, my fear of the stones. At least they let me dress. I thought that we would die together, but these men let Hamadi go. When I cried out his name, one of these men struck my face and told me to be silent. And Hamadi stole away like a thief in the early morning light, with my virtue in his palm and my heart tucked within his pocket. He did not even look back at me, this man who murmured words of love to me and proclaimed his undying devotion. But if he truly loved me, would he have left me to die alone? No. I can delude myself no longer. I know he would not. His love is a lie. My whole life is nothing but a lie.

The Pharisee yanks my arm again and I struggle to keep from falling. Anger and hatred distort the faces of these men as they drag me toward the temple and talk about their plan as if I am not present. They admit to each other that they have broken the law by letting Hamadi go, even as I have broken the law by wanting him when he was not mine to have. They have done it so they can set a trap for another. They plan to use my sin to see if this man knows the law.

As I listen, I realize their anger and hatred is not for me alone, but for Jesus of Nazareth. They want to destroy him.

I have heard of this Jesus. Who has not? Stories abound--of miracles, healings, even raising from the dead. Impossible stories. Glorious stories. Surely this worker of miracles will look upon me and instantly see the wretched sinner I have become. I cringe to think of the revulsion I will see in his eyes. Perhaps he will cast the first stone himself. Dear God in Heaven, have mercy on my wicked soul!

We have reached the temple. In my terror, I stop, and my heart pounds ever louder in my chest. If I am lucky, an early stone will strike my head and my death will be mercifully quick.

The Pharisee squeezes my arm so tight that I cry out in pain. "Silence, sinner." He spits out the words, and jerks me forward again. Only his fingers biting cruelly into my arm keep me from falling.

My accusers lead me through the large seated crowd toward the man teaching them. We stop in the midst of the crowd. I know these people wonder what I have done. Soon enough they will know. This teacher who speaks with such authority and does not pay heed to our group must be the worker of miracles. Jesus.

The senior Pharisee steps forward and calls out loudly, "Master."

Jesus turns to look at him.

"This woman was taken in adultery." The Pharisee's voice fills with disgust as he says the words which contain the trap. "In the *very act.*"

People gasp. My face burns hot with humiliation, but I stare straight ahead. Once before I saw a quiet crowd such as this get caught up in the frenzy of a stoning. I struggle to draw each breath as I wait for the first stone to sing its song of death, followed by cries of "Adulteress!" and more singing stones. My fear chokes me until I can scarcely breathe and frightened thoughts of death and eternal damnation race through my head. How many stones before the first bone is broken? How many blows will it take until I can no longer stand? How long until my fear of death changes to longing for its release?

Jesus raises his hand and the crowd quiets. My life is now reduced to just a few moments more. How long can any man stop a crowd from stoning an adulteress when the heat of self-righteousness is upon them? How long before he gives the command to begin?

One of the scribes speaks. "Now Moses in the law commandeth us, that such should be stoned: but what sayest thou?"

I have heard and so know what the Pharisees want this Jesus of Nazareth to say. They hope he says they should stone me for that will show he does not know that the law demands the man to be brought forth with the woman when caught in the act. But if he knows the law, then ... Hope flickers in my bosom, but for only a second. It matters not which way Jesus answers for either way I will be stoned. There is no hope for a sinner like me. I try to steel myself. I have not lived with much dignity. All I have left is to die with dignity.

But Jesus of Nazareth does not answer at all. Instead, he stoops to the ground and writes in the dirt as if he hasn't even heard. His hands are strong and he writes boldly, though I cannot read what he has written. He must be very learned. When my accusers persist, he finally lifts himself up, brushes the dust from his fingers, and says quietly, "He that is without sin among you, let him first cast a stone at her."

Thus Jesus of Nazareth catches the Pharisees in their sin of this trap and perhaps their own sin of adultery, of which I have also heard tales. He bends back down and writes on the ground again, completely ignoring us. I wait, gasping each breath as I wait for the stones. But there is only silence--the stones do not sing.

Suddenly, the eldest Pharisee turns and without speaking walks from the temple grounds. Then one follows another, still without a word, convicted by their own consciences, until there remains only the crowd, and Jesus of Nazareth, and an adulteress caught in the very act.

I stand still, almost in shock, and my breath is still hard to catch. Only then does Jesus stand and look around. His eyes meet mine. Nothing I have heard about this man could have prepared me for what I find there. Love shines from His eyes. Peace fills my heart. He knows what I have done--the horrible sin I have committed--and still he loves me. Love and healing and forgiveness all flow from this man who of a sudden I know is The Christ we Jews have waited for.

And His love fills my soul. My dark burden suddenly lightens and something deep within me begins to heal. Where I had expected revulsion, instead I find such compassion that I feel as if I have come home.

"Woman," Jesus asks gently, "where are thine accusers? Hath no man condemned thee?"

"No man, Lord." My voice comes out as a bare trembling whisper and my eyes brim with unshed tears.

"Neither do I condemn thee," Jesus says, and I know He speaks only the truth. "Go, and sin no more." For a moment longer his gaze locks with mine, and then he turns back to the crowd and speaks with authority. "I am the light of the world; he that followeth me shall not walk in darkness, but shall have the light of life."

Will this crowd follow Him? Or will they condemn me anew with each new day? I stand mesmerized, completely unable to move. What do I do now? Surely I am dreaming. Am I free to go? Or if I move will the crowd spring forward to stone me still?

After what seems like an eternity, an older woman struggles to her feet, approaches me and places her hand on my shoulder. "Come, sister, sit with us and learn the song of redeeming love." Her voice is also filled with this love. Others nearby nod their approval.

Now I cannot hold back my tears. I am no longer alone, but among family. Jesus of Nazareth has performed a miracle today--a miracle for me. He has changed the heart of a self-loathing sinner into that of a devoted disciple.

He has changed my life forever.

I will go and sin no more.

"But Martha was cumbered about much serving..."

*(Luke 10:40)*

# THE GOOD PART
## *Martha*

I close the door behind the messenger and shut my eyes. Jesus is coming to Bethany today. He is on his way to my home. And with Him come His disciples. In my mind, I sort through provisions to see what I can prepare on such short notice for so many men. My brother Lazarus is away, unable to even receive our guests. This, too, shall fall upon my shoulders.

I do not have a moment to waste standing about. "Mary," I call out to my sister. "Come quickly."

When Mary pokes her head around the corner, I see the concern in her eyes. "What is wrong?"

"Nothing, except thirteen men, come from instructing the seventy, who will thus be weary and in need of a meal, and we must prepare everything."

"Jesus," she guesses and her eyes shine.

I nod. "Yes, Jesus and His twelve. We will have to make space for more couches, as we only have enough for nine guests."

"Perhaps we should be glad Lazarus will not be home until later." Mary's eyes sparkle with mischief. "Or it would be fourteen men we serve." She twirls around and surveys the room. "I will clean while you cook."

I nod my agreement and smile at Mary. She is younger than I, and something of a dreamer. But when she devotes herself to a task, she works well. So we work. Sometimes Mary is in this room with me and sometimes she is not. We labor to make everything perfect for our dear friend, Jesus, and His men. While Mary rushes about, picking up everything not in its place and putting it where it belongs, dusting and washing and cleaning, I gather provisions and bring in the vegetables, and set about preparing a meal hardy enough to satisfy the appetite of thirteen hungry men and two women.

When at last Mary rejoins me to wash out her cloth, I ask, "Have you much else to do?"

"I am nearly done." She laughs softly, a joyous sound. "Unless you would have me scrub every inch twice. And see, I even remembered to wipe the dust from the window ledges." Mary turns to the table, and puts her entire body into washing it. I cannot deny that she is as excited as I am to have Jesus come to our home.

Yet my joy is overshadowed by worry. Even after I prepare this large meal, we must serve the men. With our serving girl gone until morning, it will be just Mary and myself, and we will be hard pressed to keep up with the appetites of thirteen men who have walked many miles and grown hungry.

"I love to listen to them speak," Mary says as she works her way along the table.

"He comes to speak with Lazarus," I say automatically, even though something deep inside me tells me this is not entirely true. He has spoken with the three of us on many occasions. But our culture does not recognize women as the equals of men, and women are not included in such conversations as Mary and I have had with Jesus. With Lazarus away, Jesus and His men come for rest and food. They come to our home because Lazarus is beloved of Jesus, but it will be my duty to see to their needs and serve them.

Mary pulls out our finest plates of rare wood and brings them in where I prepare the meal. "Do you believe He comes only to speak with our brother? Even after all the times He has visited and spoken with all of us as equals?"

"Lazarus is the man of the household. As a man he has need of Christ's instructions, but it would not be seemly for Jesus to come here to speak with you and me. We are meant to serve Him differently. Here in the kitchen. We shall make a meal good enough to serve a king."

"Oh, Martha, do you not ever feel the urge to drop everything and listen to Him speak? To hear His words? To feel the Holy Spirit which attends Him every moment? I know I do not wish to stay away."

"Of course I do," I say in honesty. "But what of the meal? If we leave the kitchen to listen, who will serve? And what would Jesus think of us and of Lazarus if we did?" I laugh. "We must be content as always to listen while we serve, as we come in and go out."

When I hear the sound of voices outside the door, my heart races. "It is Jesus," I say. "Yet we are not ready."

"The house looks beautiful," Mary assures me softly. "Come, let us leave our tasks and welcome our Lord."

In Lazarus' absence, it is my job as housekeeper to welcome our guests. "I will go," I say as I wipe my hands on a towel, sparing one last glance at the unfinished meal.

When I open the door, I find no surprises. The disciples speak at once, still discussing their experiences of the day. But Jesus smiles and stoops to enter. As soon as He says, "Peace be unto this house," immediately a calming peace does enter my heart.

"My Lord," I say, and welcome Him and His disciples into my home. After stepping over the threshold, He places His hands on my shoulders as He would a dear friend, and I am thankful for His friendship. Standing thus, I forget my duties for a moment and I am at peace. As I feel of My Lord's presence and His love, I wish we could stand thus forever. But of course we cannot.

Christ's gaze shifts, and I turn to find Mary kneeling before Him. He helps her up and greets her, as well.

And then the house is full of large, laughing, dusty, tired men and the burden of my duty returns. I lead them to the serving room.

Mary offers to honor our guests by washing the dust from their feet and hands, and I agree. I scan the room quickly, as the men relax against their couches, and I breathe a sigh of relief that there are now enough couches for these men and also Lazarus when he returns. As Mary begins to wash the feet of Jesus, I return to the kitchen.

I place my finest imported Italian *terra sigillata* pitcher and cups on my largest tray, and struggle to lift its weight. If only my serving girl were here to help. If only Mary were finished washing away the dust. But I am alone, so I lift the tray carefully and struggle not to spill any of the drink or break any of the pottery.

As I carry the tray to the serving room, the men talk seriously among themselves. Mary has moved on and is washing the feet of the disciples, but I can see she listens intently to their words and this *slows* her. I lower the tray to the table, and begin to serve water to the men. By the time I am done, Mary is washing the feet of yet another disciple. Yes, she works, but at such a slow pace she may never finish.

I stand and lift the now-empty tray again. As I serve, I catch snatches of conversation about the seventy who have been called and instructed this day. But I cannot stay to listen.

I return to the kitchen to refill the tray with platters of barley bread, porridge, nuts, and olives which I then carry back to the men. Mary has worked her way around much of the room, but still she washes dust away. Slowly.

"You put that lawyer in his place," Peter says, laughing. "He did not like to hear that a Samaritan could be a better neighbor than a Jew."

Jesus answers in a parable as He often does when He is teaching. I lower the tray to the table and again pass its contents among the men. I work as quickly as I can, but one woman alone serving so many takes too much time. The men are hungry, and I am anxious to serve them well and bring honor upon our house.

At last, I have served them all, yet I fear those served first will soon be ready for the next course, the one I have not yet finished.

As I lift the tray again, I check Mary's progress for I need her help desperately. I see she has only two more men's feet and hands to wash, so my spirits lift. She will help me soon.

Returning to the kitchen, I lift the lid on the pot over the fire and stir the contents. Listening for Mary to join me, I finish the dish, then remove it to separate platters for serving. But these dishes are heavy, and I dare not carry a full load this time. I put seven wooden bowls on the tray, assuring myself Mary will have completed her task and bring in the rest.

Entering the room, I see Mary washing the feet of the last man and listening to Jesus. Her efforts are distracted. A disciple calls for more wine. I serve seven of the men, and return to the kitchen for the other five plates and wine. I grow weary, but I force myself to work on.

When I re-enter the serving room, I find Mary sitting rapt at Jesus' feet, the cloth forgotten in her hand. She sits. As if there were nothing else to do. As if she cannot see I am struggling to serve so many men. As if she cares only for herself and forgets me.

What would Lazarus say if he were here and saw Mary thus? He would sit and speak with Jesus while I serve, but he is a man and that is the way of things. But women serve and *that* is also the way of things. Mary has been taught this as well as I have.

If Lazarus were here, I could ask him to remind her of her place. He would rebuke her gently and ask her to make our guests comfortable, and then to serve the meal.

Yet here she sits, and I am certain Jesus and His men will soon notice. She is showing poor training. What will Jesus think of me that I allow her to sit thus? I try to catch Mary's eye, but she does not take her gaze from Jesus' face.

Another disciple asks for bread. Growing resentful, I return to the kitchen yet again, and put loaves of freshly baked flat bread upon the tray alongside the salted fish. But still Mary sits. She listens as if she has never heard Jesus speak before. And again she does not see me.

Does Mary not realize how unfair this is to me? Does she not care what Jesus and His disciples think of us? I know how much our Lord cares for me. If anyone can tell Mary to help me, it is Jesus.

Normally, I would not involve a guest in a domestic incident, but Jesus is such a dear friend, and wise. If I ask, He will remind Mary to do her duty, and in such a way that she will not feel the chastisement of it because of His gentle loving manner. In Lazarus' absence, I turn to my friend.

Leaning the empty tray against the wall and taking a deep breath to calm myself, I say, "Lord, dost Thou not care that my sister hath left me to serve alone? Bid her therefore that she help me."

Hurt flickers across Mary's face. I know I embarrass her by pointing out her lapse before these men, friends or not, but I am tired and over warm and I do not care.

Jesus sits up on his couch, leans toward me and takes my hand in one of His. "Martha," he says. My name sounds so beautiful when He says it, as if I am the most important person on earth or in heaven. My heart eases with the security of His friendship, His caring, His love.

"Martha," He echoes. "Thou art careful and troubled about many things."

My sense of injustice begins to ease. He *can* see how Mary's idleness disturbs and burdens me, and how unfair it is.

He places His other hand on mine so that He holds my hand with His two. "But one thing is needful. And Mary hath chosen that good part, which shall not be taken away from her."

He rebukes not Mary, but myself! My face flushes hot as every pair of eyes rests upon me. If any but Jesus had spoken the words, they would have scorched my very soul. But He holds my hand still and looks with love into my eyes, and so I do not feel the reproach I would have expected. Instead, my resentment lifts, and in its place rests a new peace, a calm.

And as I gaze into His eyes, I feel the power of the man before me. The same power which convinced the fishermen in this room to leave their nets to follow Him. The same power which instructed the seventy today. The same power which heals the sick.

My mind floods with comprehension. Jesus is here so often and is such a dear friend, that I forgot who He *is*. Still He looks into my eyes, and I feel a wave of His power and divinity go through me. How could I have forgotten? I have rebuked not Mary, but my Lord and Master for allowing her to stay. I have grown so accustomed to this glorious being that I have somehow lost the wonder that once filled me. How can that be?

I remember the awe with which I viewed Him when I was baptized in His name, and I remember the vows I made that day. Even the touch of His hand on my shoulder would fill me with the power of His divinity, yet with time I have forgotten all of that. I have begun to take His words for granted. He will not be here with us always, and the realization makes my heart tighten. I have been blessed with His presence, honored to call Him friend, privileged to hear His words, yet I have lost all the wonder of it as I grow much encumbered in my own need for perfection.

Would Jesus care that my meal was not perfect? Rather He would have me honor Him by feasting upon

His word. Do I perform the proper service by allowing resentment and dissension to fill me? No. I see now that He would ask of me only to hear His message of peace and love and to take it into my heart.

Remorse fills my very soul, and tears flow down my cheeks. "My Lord," I say, and kneel at His feet while He yet holds my hand in His two. "Master." I have not honored Him. Mary washed the dust from His feet. She listened to His words and feasted on them. I thought only to tend to His hunger, and I cared much for the outward appearance of my service.

I lift my eyes to His and the power of the Holy Spirit fills me.

How clearly my thoughts come in this moment while Jesus still holds my hand. This man does not need a meal prepared for Him. He is the Christ, the very Son of God. If He grows hungry, He could change stones from our garden into bread. Yet I have much need of the meal He offers to feed my spirit.

I wanted only to serve Him, but I have forgotten His words. By so doing, have I done something akin to His refusing to eat the meal which I have prepared? He did not, but I can imagine my hurt if He did. He offers me His words lovingly, but I have been too caught up in my serving to listen. I have allowed resentment to replace love in my heart. I have hurt my sister--she whom I truly love--and I have done so, invoking the name of our Lord as my justification.

Gently Jesus pats my hand, and then lifts His hand gently to wipe away my tears. "Stay," He says, "and listen."

I cannot stop my tears until Mary puts her arm around my shoulder. On her face, there is no reproach. Just her gentle loving smile and the light of our Lord in her eyes.

Gladly, I release the burden of my tasks from my heart.

Happily, I partake of the feast The Christ offers.

Joyfully, I learn of the glories of eternity from my Lord.

I pray all may receive His words, and remember their importance.

I plead with those so blessed to take the name of our Lord upon them and to always remember Him. Take not the name of the Lord in vain, but seek always to live as He lives, to love as He loves.

He will not be here with us always as He sups this day in my very house, but His words shall never die.

I must not forget again. I must not allow the world to come between me and my Lord.

"...I have suffered
many things this day
in a dream
because of him..."

*(Matthew 27:19)*

# A NEW GOD

## *Pilate's Wife, Procula*

I have spent the morning at my usual schedule. I
have spoken with the head servants to give orders for
the evening meal. I have instructed other servants to
draw the water for my morning bath. I have lain in the
bath filled with perfumed oils and softened my skin, for
my husband is pleased by perfumes and softness.

As I rise from the bath, my chambermaids help me
dress. I do not pay attention to their idle prattle, for
they do talk much and always about inconsequential
things. Yet it is pleasant to hear the language of Rome
spoken in this foreign land. Then one mentions a man
we passed on the road a fortnight ago, he who is called
Jesus. One servant says this man has been taken before
my husband to be judged, and that the crowds are
asking for his crucifixion. This news surprises me, but I
make no comment for to speak with the servants when
they gossip is not seemly. Still, I wonder at those calling
for this Jesus to die. Surely it cannot be the same crowd
I saw with him that other day, for they seemed to be his
followers.

Crucifixion is a horribly ugly death, but certainly it
is nothing new. Normally I do not concern myself with
the affairs of my husband in ruling this province of the
empire, for he is a great man, wise and just, else why
would the gods bestow upon him the honor of ruling

this kingdom? It is not my place to concern myself in his affairs.

Yet I cannot forget the man Jesus and this troubles me. I do not allow my servants to know this, for they would carry the tale from my chambers.

I do not know what it is about the man Jesus that makes me believe he does not deserve to be crucified. I only saw him once, and that just a glance. It would not have been seemly for me to listen to him speak, but I felt a goodness about the man, even from a distance.

I feel compelled to speak with my servants, something I rarely do unless giving orders. "Is this man not the one we saw? The one in the royal lineage of the Jews?"

My maidservant nods vigorously. "Yes, my lady."

"And they want to crucify him? Is this not that same Jesus of Nazareth who you said heals people?"

"The same." My servant Flavia brushes through my hair to dress it.

Such a strange people, these Jews. Surely healing is not an act worthy of crucifixion. I would think they would wish to honor their kings and religious leaders who can do such marvelous things. It has been nigh onto seven years since my husband was assigned here, yet in all this time I do not understand these Jews.

Knowing one of my Jewish servants is a believer in this Jesus, I ask the others, "What has Halima said about this man?"

"That he is the son of their god, my Lady," another whispers loudly. The others laugh nervously.

I am more confused now than before. If this man is the son of the Jewish god, why would the Jews wish to crucify him? Surely I do not understand.

Nor do I understand why *I* am concerned for one of their spiritual leaders. I try to put him from my mind, but I cannot.

Since I am disturbed, I sit impatiently until my servants complete my hair, then I dismiss them all and enter my room of worship to pray to my gods about this man in whom I felt so much goodness.

It disturbs me to think he might be crucified, and I dislike the turmoil I feel. It will not be seemly to appear disturbed when my husband visits my chambers. He has need of me to soothe him, to provide a sanctuary from the important matters of state. He does not need to sense questions within my soul.

I open the large cupboard which houses my gods. I light incense before the image of Jupiter and another before Juno, and offer my prayers to the gods of my youth. I have been taught to seek answers from the gods, and they have never yet failed to bring me peace.

I pray for my husband to have the wisdom to make the right decision. I pray to know why Jesus concerns me. I pray that I might know what it is I should do.

I wait, but today the gods do not answer. With a sigh, I blow out the candles.

107

Still troubled, I make my way to the atrium, where I pick up my needlework. I am alone here among the growing plants, but I catch fragments of laughter and speech from elsewhere in the house.

Then I feel a presence in the room. I hear nothing, but I sense someone is here. Turning my head, I see no one. I am still alone. Yet the presence grows stronger and stronger. There is someone here.

I have never felt a presence such as this. My gods have never manifested themselves to me in this manner. A power fills the room until my arms and legs begin to tingle.

Before me, the room fades from my sight. In a dream, yet like no dream I have ever experienced before, I see a man--this same Jesus of Nazareth. Around him I see a crowd of people, as I saw him once before. As I watch, he heals one who is unclean and makes a lame girl to walk again. I cannot believe this, for it seems as though He raises a young man from the dead. Does he have power even to heal death?

I watch this man perform miracles which I have never before seen, and of a sudden I know he is a spiritual man. A Jewish prophet. I sense he is. A good man. A just man. A man such as my husband. I want to believe it is only my imagination which concocts these images I see, but they seem so real I cannot dispute them. I know he performs these miracles by the power of the Jewish god, as I know I am shown this waking dream through the same power. Who is this

Jesus? And what is he to the Jewish god? Is he truly his son?

The crowd around Jesus suddenly changes, and I know these people are not his followers. Except one man who comes smiling and kisses Jesus.

I watch as my husband's soldiers, taking a cue from the smiling one, seize Jesus. This Jesus of Nazareth has been betrayed with the kiss of a friend. He is taken before my husband, Pilate. To my horror, I see my husband allow him to be condemned to death by crucifixion.

In this dream, which is not a dream, I know with all certainty that this man is guilty of no crime. I know he is pure as no man I have ever seen. How can it be possible that he is this pure? He is innocent. This I know with a surety.

Why am I being shown this dream? Am I to tell Pilate? Jesus is not my concern. What has he to do with me, the wife of Pilate? I do not concern myself with the affairs of state, only with the management of the household. Since the Jewish people sent the formal protest to Rome about my husband's actions, Pilate has been wary and careful in his judgments, lest there be more trouble. No, I dare not intervene.

Any questions I had before now fade as I see my husband's soldiers lay Jesus upon a cross. My breath catches in my throat as they place the tip of a spike against his hand and raise a mallet.

Many of my people go to see the crucifixions, but I have always shrunk from going. Pilate has allowed me this one small indulgence and has since sought to spare me the sight of such a death. Because of this, I have imagined much, but in this strange reality it is a hundredfold worse than I ever imagined.

As my husband's soldier swings the mallet against the spike, metal rings against metal. The ringing sickens me, but again the soldier strikes, and again, and again. Blood flows from the wound, and I recoil from the horror, yet the image does not fade. People who love him gather around the cross. They suffer and cry out in their grief, and my heart is filled with sadness for them.

I cannot bear this, even in my dream. I close my eyes, but the scene is still before me. I cover my ears, but I still hear the mallet striking, striking, striking, until spikes are driven through Jesus' hands and wrists and feet.

Tears fill my eyes as I see the crown of thorns upon his head. My husband's soldiers lift up the cross and jeer at the man Jesus as he hangs there. They mock him while he bleeds, while the life slowly drains from him, and I am sickened to my very soul to see my people treating this good man so.

Why must Jesus die such a death, and what shall my husband suffer if this dream comes to pass? What reproach will he heap upon himself if he learns too late the man Jesus is a good and innocent man?

At last, the dream fades. I take a deep, sobbing breath and try to stand, but my limbs are weak and I fear I will fall. Carefully, anxious to leave this room and this horrible dream, I stumble into my bed chamber and lie upon my bed to recover.

But even there I cannot escape the memory. The dream torments me. The horrible ringing of the mallet on the spike haunts me. The blood of an innocent man tortures me.

What does the dream mean and why was it shown to me? What does the god of the Jews want me to do? I cannot influence my husband on the judgment seat. He would never allow it. For my husband to accept my influence would imply weakness; for me to offer would imply doubt in his wisdom. I have never done so before. I cannot do it now.

Yet no sooner have I decided thus then the dream begins again. This time, while the man is on the cross, one of my husband's soldiers places a sponge with vinegar upon his parched and bleeding lips, and I cry again as I sense his suffering. Why do I cry for this man? For this Jew?

While his other followers stand a ways off, one woman sits at his feet and weeps.

As I weep also, Jesus looks down and his eyes meet mine. Nothing has prepared me for the power of his gaze. Bruised, bleeding, dying, yet he has power such as I have never felt. And a love fills me unlike anything I have ever known. I cannot even attempt to describe it.

"Come, follow me," I hear the words as though he speaks, and they pull at my heart. Then he lifts his eyes from mine and gazes to the heavens, and I am left shaken and weak.

I hear him say, "Father, forgive them, for they know not what they do." How can he do that? How can he be so noble? I can scarcely comprehend it. I am in awe that he could suffer this torture and still utter these words.

On his cross, Jesus cries out, "It is finished. Father, into thy hands I commend my spirit." And as I watch in horror, his head drops to his chest and he gives up his life. In this, I perceive he truly had power over death. Surely he could have raised himself as he did the young man.

Then I realize he addressed the Jewish god as Father. Before I can ponder this, the earth begins to shake. I know not if it shakes just in my dream, but I grab hold of my bed to keep from falling. It is as if the earth itself is sorrowing. I see my husband's soldiers cower in fear, I hear the weeping of Jesus' followers, and hear one of my husband's centurions cry out. "Truly," he says, "this was the Son of God."

At long last, the earth stops shaking, but my thoughts continue to swirl. I understand not how this god, for which the Jews refuse to make an image, can have a son in the image of a man. But I cannot deny what I have seen and heard. I cannot deny that this

Jesus is very important to his god. And my good and noble husband will be responsible for his horrible death.

As the dream fades before me, I know what I must do. That which I have feared to do. I must send a message to warn Pilate. He must not let this crucifixion be carried out.

I am surprised to see my room is as it was before. Though the earth seemed to shake under my very feet, nothing is out of place.

Again I hesitate. I risk raising my husband's ire, or worse, of humiliating him publicly. Neither would I willingly do, yet I am compelled to send a message to my husband before he can commit this serious error.

This man Jesus is not as ordinary men, as the Jewish god is not as ordinary gods, but one filled with all power. I know not whether Jesus is truly the son of this god, but I do know he is beloved and important to his god.

Trembling, I reach for a piece of parchment on which to write. I do so knowing I overstep my place, that I might be harming my relationship with my husband, yet I dare not ignore what the god of the Jews wants me to do. I choose my words carefully, remembering that Pilate might not understand or even believe what I have seen. Finally, I write, *Have thou nothing to do with that just man: for I have suffered many things this day in a dream because of him.*

I seal the parchment and call for Pilate's trusted centurion, Marcus. Handing him the note, I tell him to take it straightway to my husband. I know word of my sending this note could easily spread, but I cannot help that.

"He is on the judgment seat," the centurion protests. He does not approve of my intervention, I can see that. But I no longer care.

"I know," I say, "but he must receive this missive." I harden my tone. "Take it immediately. Do not fail me, for I shall not take failure lightly."

Now the centurion nods sharply. "Yes, Lady Procula. I will do this thing you have asked." He smites his breast in salute. I know he is displeased, but I know he will do this thing though he does not agree with it.

As he leaves, I take a deep breath to steady myself. I have done all I can. Now I must hope Pilate will do the right thing with the man Jesus.

Near desperation, I return to my room of worship to burn more incense to the gods and to again ask Jupiter to help. But I pause at the entrance to the room which has always provided me with peace. Of a sudden it does not seem right to plead this cause with Jupiter.

A chill runs through me as I think of the Jewish god. The god to which the Jews refuse to give form or substance. The dream he sent me today was so vivid and even now my soul is filled with an intensity I have never felt before. I am afraid Pilate will not receive my note in time, or that he might ignore my plea, but underlying my fear is a strange peace. One which makes me realize my other gods have never truly given me peace, rather only satisfaction.

In that moment, I do something I have not done since I learned to pray to my gods as a child. I rearrange the space in my cupboard of worship to make a space for a new god, a more powerful god than I have worshiped before.

I will place no image in this space which I have cleared, but will honor the Jewish god, as his followers do, by not providing a form for him.

I light another candle and place it before the empty space of this new god. I offer a prayer to this god with no image and plead with him to protect these just men, my husband, and the man Jesus. Of a sudden a calmness enter my heart. I am assured that I did what this Jewish god asked of me, and he is pleased that I obeyed.

I know the Jewish god would not allow this horrible death to happen to his son unless it was meant to be. And, as if someone speaks to my heart, I know that whatever happens now, whatever Pilate decides, everything is as it must be.

"Woman,
why weepest thou?"

*(John 20:15)*

# HE IS RISEN!
## *Mary Magdalene*

I walk slowly up the hill to the sepulchre where they laid my Lord after His death. Jesus was buried with such haste on the eve of the Sabbath, that I go now to ensure all of the preparations were handled properly. I perform my last service for my Lord this morning by bringing sweet spices that I might anoint Him.

I want also to make sure no harm came to His body when the great earthquake--yet another sign of our Father's displeasure at the rejection of His Son--shook the earth in the night. As I walk, I struggle to hold back the tears which have overwhelmed me since my beloved Jesus suffered and died on the cross.

Mary, the mother of the apostle James, walks before me. Salome, the mother of the apostles John and the other James, is at my side. Joanna comes behind me. Yet I am alone in the magnitude of my grief.

We travel silently and carefully along the path. It has shifted since the earthquakes, and I must concentrate to keep from falling in the darkness. Yet even this simple task of walking is made difficult by the refusal of my thoughts to stay anywhere but with Jesus. Haunted by the memory of Him hanging on the cross, I rub my forehead with my hand as though that could wipe the awful image from my mind.

I knelt at His very feet as He hung there. As He suffered and died. My heart wrenches as I think of His torn and bleeding body and of the majesty of His voice as He pled with our Father to forgive the soldiers.

And now He is gone. My healer. My teacher. My friend. The one I love beyond measure.

Following Mary up the stony path toward the sepulchre, I wonder what I am to do now. I have followed Jesus since He saved my soul and cast the seven devils out from me. I have forsaken all--family and friends and possessions--to follow Him. Yet I have gained so much more than I ever lost because of His great love for me and mine for Him. Even with the pain I now feel, I would do the same again.

I have walked many miles with him over the past three years. I have witnessed so many marvelous miracles. I sat at His feet and listened to His voice as He unfolded the mysteries of eternity.

*These* are the memories I wish to remember. Jesus showed such compassion to the widows and orphans. He laid His hands on the lame and the lepers and the blind and they dropped their staffs and walked, and they became whole, and they looked upon the world around them for the first time. He turned water to wine, five fishes into a meal for five thousand, guilt-ridden hearts into hearts of disciples.

Especially I cherish the memory of the children. They thronged to Jesus, drawn more strongly than even the adults by His sweet, strong, loving spirit. He would sit with them, touch their cheeks, pat their heads and pull them close to speak with them. With no children of His own, they were all His children, and He showered His love upon them.

I trip over a stone and fling out my arm to catch my balance. There is no one who can ever take Jesus' place. No one with His compassion, His power, His wisdom. No one to love me as He does. No one to follow. To comfort. To serve. No one to make me smile. To make me feel alive. Even in quiet moments, when neither of us spoke, I was content.

Without Him here, I fear I shall wither and blow away in the wind. But I cannot. I must do as He asked of me and hope one day my will to live might return, for the pain of my loss is so great it could drive me to the earth if I let it.

I have never been sorry for my decision to follow Jesus. My only regret is that I had no chance to bid Him farewell before He was betrayed and seized by the soldiers, before the horrible mockery He endured, before His torture, death, and burial.

I could not leave Jesus as He hung on the cross. So great was His suffering I could scarcely bear to witness it, yet I could not leave His side. The other women all stood far off, but my grief was so great I would have suffered alone even if they stood beside me, and my devotion to my Master compelled me to remain at His feet. And though my eyes watched Him die, my heart refuses to believe He is no longer here. Perhaps if I could see His body once more, I could deal with this horrible pain which has kept me from sleep and from food and from peace since He was crucified.

Jesus tried to explain to me what must happen, but I never thought He would suffer so. His pain tore my own heart as I knelt under the cross and saw the blood drip from His body.

Now He is gone, and my heart is like a great stone in my chest. Only those places inside where I feel that I, too, have died are free from this unbearable pain.

My heart breaks again and tears flood my eyes. "Why did not Jesus command the hosts of Heaven to save Himself?" I ask aloud as though my pain must find words. "He could have stopped everything. Why did He not?"

With my outburst, the other women stop. Salome wraps her arms around me and says, "He did our Father's will."

"But He had the power to command even the wind and the waves to obey His will. He saved others from death. Why did He meekly hang and allow them to sacrifice Him?"

Salome brushes my hair back from my forehead. "Mary, you know this was His mission. His destiny. This is why He came to earth."

"But I miss Him so," I whisper. I lay my head on Salome's shoulder as she continues to murmur words of comfort. Despite my grief, I know in my heart she is right. After a moment, when I can at last raise my head, we continue our journey.

He did our Father's will. And I must do the same. In the weeks and months before His death, we spoke often. I have listened to Him and watched Him. It is the Father's sweet, simple message which Jesus shared with others, through His words and through the example of His life. The whole of it can be expressed in one word. Love. All else He asks of us is encompassed therein.

So I will begin by anointing the body of my Lord, and then I will prayerfully search out other opportunities to serve others with love. I will do that which my Father wishes me to do.

Mary asks, "Who shall roll us away the stone from the door of the sepulchre?"

My footsteps falter. I would despair at her question, yet I have nothing left to despair over a stone. I saw the difficulty with which the soldiers rolled it into place. They were healthy, robust men and there were many of them. I know not how we will move it, for it is great, and there are few of us women. Somehow I must have faith that God will provide the way. I drag in a ragged breath and utter a prayer.

As we near the tomb, Mary gasps and turns to me. Beyond her, I see the sepulchre and realize, as she does, that the large stone has already been moved aside. The others hesitate on the trail, indecision evident on their faces. Yet why do they hesitate? God has answered our prayers to move the stone. Now I can anoint the body of Jesus, my Lord, my Savior.

121

My eyes scan the massive round stone as I near it. I stop for suddenly I see two strange men sitting on top of it. An overwhelming fear chills me as I step past them toward the sepulchre. Looking beyond them, I see that the bed on which we laid Jesus' body is empty.

Jesus is gone. The tomb is empty save for the robes in which He was wrapped. Fear makes my hands tremble even as despair threatens to overwhelm my grief. These men do not look like Roman soldiers, yet who else would they be? They do not wear the robes of the Pharisees, yet could they be hirelings? Many vile and wicked people wish my Lord ill. But would they carry their hatred so far they would steal His body?

I stand, unable to move, fearful, angry and defeated by this latest display of hatred. Yet even more painful than wondering who took my Lord's body, is the despair caused by the simple fact that He is gone.

One of the men holds my gaze and asks, "Why seek ye the living among the dead? He is not here, but is risen. Remember how He spake unto you when He was yet in Galilee, saying The Son of Man must be delivered into the hands of sinful men, and be crucified, and the third day rise again."

He is not here. At the man's words, my heart feels as if it will break in two. He is not here. They have taken His body. Who are these men who mock Jesus' promise to rise again? What manner of men could conceive of stealing Jesus' body from the tomb? Have they not done enough?

Joanna wraps her robes tightly about her. "We must find Peter," she says, and then she turns to go back, half-running.

I turn away, too numb to feel more, but still the pain tears at my chest. Jesus is not here. I cannot perform even one last service for my Lord.

I stumble down the broken trail and endless tears blur my vision. My hands and legs tremble so that I can scarcely walk. Salome turns to make sure I am still behind them, as if she senses how close I am to collapse

*He is not here.*

I barely see the ground or the other women because of my tears and my pain. When we reach the house, we burst in upon the apostles without knocking. They sit in silence, much troubled by the crucifixion of our Lord and Master. I stand back, unable to speak, and let the other women tell them what we saw and heard. But their tale seems to the apostles as idle words and the men believe them not.

Do they think we are imagining? Or so far gone in our grief we know not what we see? I clutch Peter's sleeve and force my voice to a semblance of calm. "They have taken away the Lord out of the sepulchre, and we know not where they have laid Him."

My words seem to move Peter as those of the other women did not. His eyes grow angry and his jaw hard. He is ready, I see, to protect the body of Jesus. He summons John, he who was also beloved of Jesus, and together they rush from the house toward the sepulchre.

I cannot help but follow. Peter seeks to spare me the anguish of going, but when I insist he agrees.

They are angry, these great men who love Jesus and gave all to serve Him, and so their pace is quick. The way is easier now that it is light, yet I must hurry to match their long, deliberate strides.

I look back once to see the other women standing before the house. They may tarry there out of fear, but I must know for certain what has happened to my master.

As we near the tomb, I say, "There were two men sitting on the stone." But when we arrive, the men are no longer there. I wait what seems like forever while Peter and John look inside the sepulchre. When they return, I ask, "Are the men still there?"

Peter shakes his head. The pain in his eyes mirrors my own. "There is no one inside."

"What of Jesus' body?" I ask.

Peter turns to go. "His body is gone. Only the robes remain."

"He is gone." Awe fills John's eyes and his voice as he repeats what everyone has said before.

He is gone. I will never see Him again. I suppress a wounded cry.

Peter asks me to return with him and John, but I cannot. As I watch them leave, my tears begin again, nearly choking me now that I stand alone before the sepulchre. A need grows within me to touch at least the cloth that bound His body. Perhaps then I will feel His presence and find the comfort I need.

I take a deep breath, then walk slowly past the large stone. Stooping down, I peer into the sepulchre, intending to let my eyes adjust to the dim light before I enter. But the tomb is not dark, nor is it empty. The two men I saw earlier are still there. Why is it I can see them when even Peter and John cannot? They sit where the body of Jesus should have been--one at the head and the other at the foot. My pain sharpens and threatens to steal away my very breath. I am exhausted. I can take no more. My tears flow with abandon.

One of the men asks me, "Woman, why weepest thou?" As he speaks, I marvel at the caring I sense in his voice.

Defeated, I say, "Because they have taken away my Lord and I know not where they have laid Him." My voice cracks on the words and I can scarce speak.

The Holy Spirit sweeps through me and leaves my limbs tingling. Suddenly I know without doubt who these two men dressed in shining garments are--not ordinary men, but angels. And then I know also that it was neither Roman soldiers nor Pharisee hirelings who took Jesus' body. Angels have taken Jesus to our Father. When Jesus foretold He would rise again on the third day, He knew the angels would come for His body. Doubtless His spirit is already with His Father.

Grief and loneliness overwhelm me. I stumble a few steps and fall against the large stone. My shoulders shudder in full heavy sobs. Oh, please, my God, help me, for I cannot bear this. The loss is too great.

I hear footsteps behind me, and turn to see who has come to grieve with me. Through my tear-filled eyes, I see a gardener, who asks the same question as the angel: "Woman, why weepest thou?"

I am sobbing so hard I cannot reply. I rub my eyes with the skirt of my robe and try to wipe the endless flow of tears from my cheeks.

Then, more gently, the man asks, "Whom seekest thou?"

Moments pass before I am able to speak, and then I beseech him. "Sir, if thou have bourne Him hence, tell me where thou hast laid Him, and I will take Him away."

"Mary," the man says softly.

That voice. At the familiar sound, my heart leaps with joy. Oh, how could I not have recognized my Lord? His gentle smile. His strength. His love. Was it only that I did not expect to see Him thus? His spirit looks as His body did before. And then immediately I realize I am wrong. This cannot be His spirit only, for the marks of His death are imprinted on His hands and feet. The sight of those horrible wounds causes my breath to catch in my throat and a knot of pain to fill my heart.

Yet I see they are now a symbol of His sacrifice so that all may know Him for who He is. Jesus, the Christ, the Lamb of God. My Lord stands before me, resurrected as He said He would be, but I knew not how it would be accomplished. I had not expected His body to rise, but only His spirit to rise to join His Father. Yet as I gaze upon my Lord's familiar features and the hands that so often lay gently upon my head as He blessed me or soothed trouble from my brow, I see how weak my understanding was.

*He* has taken up His body. *He* has risen. He *did* command the very powers of Heaven, not to save Himself from the cross, but to overcome it.

My tears increase an hundred fold, but this time they are in gratitude that my Lord has returned.

"Rabboni," I cry out. "Master." The joy in my heart vibrates in my voice.

Jesus smiles, the most gentle of smiles, and I can do naught but fall to the ground at His feet and worship Him.

He reaches out a hand toward me and I rise to my feet, and the peace that always comes when I am near Him envelopes my heart and warms my soul. He looks different to me already. His new glory is already descending upon Him. His hair is now a celestial white and light surrounds His body. I marvel at the wounds upon His hands. *He lives.* It is another miracle, and this is the greatest of all I have seen Jesus perform.

My Lord stands before me, and I see that our friendship is older than time and will continue forever. Mere death cannot end our earthly friendship. I can reach out and touch Him once again.

"Hold me not," Jesus says, "for I am not yet ascended to my Father."

As I hear Jesus' gentle words, I sense our Father waits, as does the glory that is to be Jesus', and so I cannot ask Him to tarry. I know of His suffering in the garden. I know of the persecution He endured. In Pilate's court and on the cross. Now that His mission is completed, He can take His place at His Father's side. Only His compassion at my grief keeps Him here now.

At last, the warmth I always feel in His presence calms me and I am able to stop my tears. "You must go again," I somehow manage to whisper.

He does not look away, but nods gently.

How can I let Him leave again? *Please, my God, give me the strength to do Thy will.* I must say goodbye, yet in my woman's heart alone I cannot find the way. I know at once that our Father has heard me, for an overwhelming sense of peace fills me.

With this added strength beyond my own, I am able to force my voice not to waver. "I am ready," I say, though I might never be.

He smiles again. "But go to my brethren, and say unto them, I ascend unto my Father, and your Father." He points to the heavens in a majestic gesture, full of power and life. "And to my God, and your God."

I manage to whisper, "Farewell," before I turn away, as I know I must.

Holding my head high, I resist the tears that threaten to return when Jesus cannot see, and I follow the stony trail away from my Lord. I have not gone far when the Holy Spirit again sweeps through my entire body, and my limbs weaken with the truth spreading through them. This is my confirmation that that which Jesus has prophesied has come to pass. I do not look back, for I know He will not be there if I do. He has gone, ascended to His Father and my Father, His God and my God.

My knees weaken and I kneel on the path to thank God for this last moment with my Lord and for the strength to do what He bid me. I am alone, yet peace grows in my heart, nestled within the pain. I am alone, yet I know I will never truly be alone again, for God comforts me. I have been truly blessed among women. I was chosen--before His mother or Peter or any other--to be the first witness of His resurrection. And though Jesus is gone from among us, His presence and peace will be with me always.

I must share this new knowledge I have been given with the others, for they will be as comforted as I am to understand--at last--our Father's promise of resurrection.

I stand once more and lift up my face to the warmth of the sun, and feel one more promise imprint itself upon my soul.

When it is my Father's will that I leave this earth, Jesus will be there to greet me, dressed in robes of brightest glory.

And on that day I will feel only joy.

# AUTHOR'S NOTE

I hope that you have gained as much joy from reading these stories as I have from putting them on paper for you. I hope you have found yourself being drawn closer to our Savior as you read. And I hope we can share Jesus' love-filled light with others as we heal through the Atonement of Christ.

I have worked hard to keep these stories scripturally and historically accurate, to add details of life in Christ's time, and to gain more understanding of the women and stories themselves.

The only change I have made to the scriptural accounts is in Anna's story. Simeon actually saw and held Jesus first and spoke his words before Anna came into the courtyard of the temple, and, since I wanted to show his words and actions through Anna's eyes, I have Anna entering earlier and holding Jesus first.

If I have named any of these women, it is because their name is given in the scriptures or I found it in a corroborating source (as with Pilate's wife, Procula). I did give names to other people in these stories to add reality to the narrative. Servants (Flavia, Halima). A son (Lateef). A daughter (Yalena). Friends (Yahra, Mareshah). A betrothed (Omner). Others (Hamadi, Rashidi).

Though the story of Christ's earthly life and ministry officially ends with Mary Magdalene's story of Christ's resurrection, I have included two bonus stories in this volume.

The first, *For This Reason Have I Come*, is one I feel completes the WOMEN WHO KNEW story; however, it is significantly different in a couple of ways from the others and so I did not include it above. Though the story of the events is based on ancient accounts, the woman is not an actual woman in scriptures, as are all the others, and the account is not from the New Testament, as are all the others.

When Christ comes again, He will come in glory and everyone on earth will know Him and acknowledge who He is. There is an awesome account of Christ appearing--in glory, just as He will in the Second Coming--in *The Book of Mormon, Another Testament of Jesus Christ*, an account of the Native Americans for many generations, including at the time of Christ's life and crucifixion. This story is based on that account.

I know when Christ visits this earth again, at His Second Coming, He will come in glory, just as He appeared to the Nephites. And then, through the divinity and love of Christ, our Shepherd, we shall all truly become one fold. And we may each have the opportunity to look into Christ's eyes and see the love He has for us, and be healed.

I have also included a preview from the upcoming companion volume to this book, MEN WHO KNEW: *The Mortal Messiah* . The story I have chosen to share is the wonderful one of Peter's walk upon the waves, entitled *A Little Faith*.

# WOMEN WHO KNEW

# BONUS STORY

"And other sheep I have,
which are not of this fold,
they also
shall hear my voice,
and there shall be
one fold,
and one shepherd."

*(John 10:16)*

# FOR THIS REASON
# HAVE I COME
## *Nephite Woman*

"Your stitches need to be smaller and neater, Safiya," Mother admonishes me. "The way Jamila used to do them." As she speaks, I see the familiar sadness fall upon her. The official mourning period for my beautiful sister ended over a year ago. To the rest of the city it is now as if she never existed. Yet, in my home, she is always between my mother and me. While she lived I was never so good as she was. And now that she is gone Mother spends so much time still mourning Jamila that at times it seems she does not see me or my younger brother.

Sighing, I examine the wedding gift I prepare for Omner. Not for the first time, I wish I had talents as plentiful as my sister was blessed with. No, my stitches are not so fine as Jamila's, but then no one else could do them so fine. Still, my work is good, and resentment rises within me at my mother's blindness to my own abilities. "I am not Jamila."

"Well, nonetheless," Mother continues. "This is what any man wants in a wife. Someone who makes fine stitches, and runs a household well and fills his belly."

I know that with each statement Mother compares me with Jamila and finds me wanting. I know how painful it is for her to make wedding preparations for me to wed Omner. Harder still to have me put on the wedding dress sewn for Jamila and alter it before my wedding day in another fortnight. Two years ago Jamila was to be Omner's bride. Now, because of the alliance desired between our families, I am to take her place.

But Mother's pain seems small to me when I wonder how Omner feels to have me for a bride. I brush away the thought for I have loved Omner always and I cannot bear to think of him loving another more than me, even my beautiful sister.

Mother stands in the corner that used to be Jamila's and opens the cupboard which has been kept as it was before she died. Mother fingers the wedding dress and bursts into tears. I wish she and Father could forget Jamila, even if only for short periods of time. I wish I could. I wish God had taken me instead of her, for that would have spared us all so much pain. As Mother struggles to regain her composure, I set aside my inadequate needlework.

Sighing, I cross the room and put my hand on Mother's arm to calm her. She smiles genuinely now and I feel her love for me, though I know her smile will quickly fade with her still-fresh grief for her favored daughter.

While Jamila grew more and more sick, I prayed that God would spare her. I have been taught stories of God and of His Son, Jesus Christ, my whole life. Many times have my parents told me what the scriptures say of Jesus and how He would heal the sick and raise the dead. But He did not heal Jamila, and He did not raise her from the dead, though I prayed every day that He would.

So on the day Jamila's body was placed into the ground, I did not pray. And I have not prayed since. For Mother's and Father's and Omner's sake, I pretend to pray, but I do not. Not to a God who does not listen and does not care. Not to a God who takes innocent pure people and leaves prayers unanswered.

I force my thoughts away from my hurt and my anger. I have never revealed this anger to anyone, for I know to be angry at God is a sin. And I will never share this secret with Mother or Father or Omner, for I could not bear to see their disappointment. I would not wish to live if Omner were to cancel our betrothal because of my sins. And I can barely admit to myself my unloving thoughts toward my God.

Without warning, a flash of sharp lightning illuminates the room. Thunder follows almost immediately, thunder that shakes the earth as if it is about to divide asunder. My eyes meet Mother's and I am sure mine must be as wide and terrified as hers. When the earth begins to shake, I quake with fear and struggle to remain standing.

Terrified, Mother screams as she falls to the ground. I reach out for her, but the earth shifts beneath my feet and I fall and bruise my hip. The earth still shakes so badly that Mother and I are forced to brace ourselves just to balance on the floor.

"We must see if the others are hurt." The fear in Mother's voice matches that in my heart, for my brother is only seven and Grandmother Benu is so old a fall could hurt her badly. Over the almost continuous din of crashing thunder, we call out until we hear them answer in the next room, but it seems to take us an eternity to crawl across the shifting floor. They are scratched and bruised, as are we, but otherwise not harmed.

Somewhere behind me, I hear the sound of our pottery crashing to the ground. Through the doorway, I see lightning the size of a giant tree blaze to the earth. It strikes a house up the road and a fire begins. The thunder causes the earth to shake even harder.

A thin, long crack opens in the floor beneath us. I gasp and scramble backward to the wall. Outside, the destruction is even greater, and an entire house falls into the earth.

"What manner of storm is this?" Mother cries out in terror.

"This is no storm," I say. "A storm does not swallow houses." Surely this is the end of the world. Perhaps we will all die this day.

I huddle with the others in our main room, hoping the house will not collapse, much of the time holding hands, and crying. The crack opens wider and one wall leans slightly. The smell of smoke from the other house which is on fire singes my nostrils and burns my throat.

The sun has passed far in the sky, so I know this

horrible destruction has been going on for several hours. Will it continue until all our houses are swallowed up and we are all dead? Just as I begin to believe this terror will never end, the earth stops shaking. The constant lightning and thunder lessen, now only occasionally striking the earth.

Fear chokes me and I wonder where Father is at this moment. Because he walks with a limp, this shaking earth will be hard for him to traverse.

And where is Omner? I scarcely dare think of him, for if anything should happen to him I could not bear it. Will he go to his home first, or will duty make him stop here to see to my safety? I do not know. I can only wait.

Still choking on the dust and smoke in the air, I help Grandmother off the floor. After so much noise and confusion, the near quiet seems unreal to me--the earth has rocked to and fro now for so long that it seems almost strange to find myself on ground that does not sway beneath me. Yet it still trembles beneath my feet. I realize it is not entirely quiet for the earth still groans as if in pain.

Not long after the shaking stops, my father stumbles through the door. Tears of gratitude for his safety flow down my cheeks as we all throw our arms around him, grateful he is home. Yet with fear in my heart, I ask, "Did you see Omner? Is he safe?"

"I do not know, Safiya," Father hugs me tight. "We can only pray for him, and thank the Lord for delivering us."

Father motions to us, and we all kneel. I listen as he prays, but I do not close my eyes. Thus am I the first to see the darkness, a terrible black fog, as it rolls toward the house. I gasp aloud with panic, and the others open their eyes. Unable even to speak, I simply point out the window, and they all gaze in horror at the fog which creeps into the house, enveloping everything in its path and dividing me from the others. In only moments we are surrounded by a darkness so black I cannot see anything--not even my hand before my face.

I cry out, as do the others, and I clutch my Grandmother's hand for comfort. My eyes sting and my throat burns from the vapor. Grandmother pulls my head down into her lap, and rubs my forehead, and her simple loving touch calms me in my terror. She hums a familiar lullaby, and I cry.

Thunder crashes again, yet I cannot see the lightning through this thick blackness which surrounds us. It is yet day and the darkness which has fallen is unlike any night I have ever experienced.

I hear the sound of someone shuffling around on the floor and I call out, "Who is that? Where are you going?"

Father calmly tells us he will make a fire to penetrate the darkness and give us some heat, and now I recognize the familiar sounds. I see no light, but the smell of smoke grows stronger and I cry out again in terror. Did Father's fire begin and does it now spread throughout the house? Father assures us he was not able to start a fire, but my heart races. If I cannot see fire, how can I escape being burned?

I cannot see Father but I hear him pray for our deliverance and safety. Then he prays for Omner, and in my fear I hope the Lord has kept Omner safe. But the faith I lost on the day of Jamila's burial will not return so easily. I wish I could believe. But I do not.

We sit in this inky dark and breathe dust and smoke. Father tries to teach us as he always does. He reminds us of the prophet, Samuel the Lamanite, who prophesied of the death of Jesus Christ. He says the darkness and the shaking earth are signs to tell us Jesus has died in the land our Father Lehi left many centuries before I was born. I have heard the prophecies before, but never did I imagine anything so terrifying as this.

The earth shudders again and the wall shifts behind me. Something heavy hits my leg and breaks. I cry out in my pain. I feel moisture on my leg so I know I am bleeding, but I cannot see. I take my dress and hold it against my leg and hope the bleeding stops.

I hear the screams of fear and cries of mourning from people in other houses. Father speaks on, halting only when a cry rises too loud to ignore. Is this how this angry God gives signs? By taking more people away from those who love them?

I do not know how long it has been dark because I have lost all sense of time. We have sat thus, unable to see even a shadow, for ever. When Mother asks, Father guesses it has been a day and a night. So long to be frightened. To feel lost and alone. Again, I wonder at a God who would frighten us so.

I want to run, to find someplace with light, some place where wails of mourning do not pierce the quiet. But there is no longer such a place, even if I could see to find it.

My mouth is dry with dust. My brother cries from hunger and thirst and fear, and my own stomach growls.

As I hold Grandmother Benu's trembling hand, a voice fills the darkness. Not a normal voice. A quiet voice, yet so powerful and penetrating that it cuts through to my very soul.

"Wo, wo, wo unto this people," says the voice in sadness. "Wo unto the inhabitants of the whole earth except they shall repent; for the devil laugheth, and his angels rejoice, because of the slain of the fair sons and daughters of my people; and it is because of their iniquity and abominations that they are fallen!

"Behold, that great city Zarahemla have I burned with fire, and the inhabitants thereof. And behold, that great city Moroni have I caused to be sunk in the depths of the sea, and the inhabitants thereof to be drowned." As the voice pronounces that these people were wicked and so now they are all dead, my hurt, anger and fear intensify. God the Father is angry His son has been killed. My own thoughts have been wicked since Jamila died. My heart has been as stone in my anger at God. I clutch Grandmother's hand, terrified to realize my iniquities might cause me and those I love to suffer.

"And, behold," the voice says. "The city of Gilgal have I caused to be sunk, and the inhabitants thereof to be buried up in the depths of the earth."

I tremble and try to move closer to the wall as if it could save me. My cousin lived in Gilgal, but the city has been sunk. Outside, there arises a cry from many people of "Oh, that we had repented before this destruction." Mother and Father take up the lament.

Mother, Father, Grandmother Benu and even my little brother raise their voices again in prayer, but I cannot. I will not. I fear if God hears my voice it will only serve to remind Him to destroy me with the rest of the wicked. How can I turn to Him for help?

The voice goes on and on, and my fear turns to terror as the voice lists city after city which has been buried with water, or buried with earth, or burned with fire. City after city after city, hundreds of thousands of people, all destroyed.

"O all ye that are spared because ye were more righteous than they, will ye not now return unto me, and repent of your sins, and be converted, that I may heal you?"

My heart leaps, yet I am surprised. For just a moment I wish it could be as the voice has said. That I could repent and be healed. Yet these sins of which the

143

voice speaks must be minor, of no real account. Perhaps an idle afternoon spent gossiping by the well or a simple transgression. But surely not the coldness of heart or the anger with which I have felt toward God since Jamila's death.

"Behold," says the voice, "I am Jesus Christ, the Son of God...I was with the Father from the beginning...I am the light and the life of the world."

This Christ is a vengeful God, and the angry Son of a vengeful Father. He claims He is the light, yet He speaks in the midst of a darkness I have never before seen. He claims to be the life of the world, yet He destroys thousands of people. I do not understand this kind of life and light.

"...And ye shall offer for a sacrifice unto me a broken heart and a contrite spirit. Behold, I have come unto the world to bring redemption unto the world, to save the world from sin. Therefore, whoso repenteth and cometh unto me as a little child, him will I receive, for of such is the kingdom of God. Behold, for such I have laid down my life, and have taken it up again; therefore repent, and come unto me ye ends of the earth, and be saved."

I wish I could repent. Yet will He accept repentance born of fear? No, I think not. I cannot repent while I yet feel my anger through my fear.

Christ's voice ceases, and in the stillness that follows I realize that even the wailing of the mourners has stopped. Still I sit beside my family.

Always I touch someone for reassurance and comfort, leaning against Father's strong shoulders, rubbing the material of Grandmother Benu's skirt between my fingers, comforting my brother by rubbing his forehead as Grandmother rubbed mine, putting my arm around Mother's shoulders.

I sleep fitfully now and then, having lost all sense of time and awake to the sounds of weeping and wailing that has begun once again in the houses around ours.

Finally, a faint glimmer of light cuts through the darkness. The others see it as well, for they cry out in relief as do I. The heavy black fog disperses as the light of the sun burns through, and I see with wonder the most glorious sunrise I have ever seen.

The earth ceases to tremble and the rocks to rend. The dreadful groanings cease and all the tumultuous noise passes away. Tears of gratitude fall down my cheeks for this new day. Never has the sun seemed more beautiful. With wonder, I listen to a bird sing for the first time since the destruction began.

I climb to my feet, and stretch my body. My leg burns where it was cut, and my muscles are bruised and sore. I help Grandmother Benu up, and lift an overturned chair for her to sit in. My brother holds tight to Father's side.

Only now do I see the extent of the devastation around us. I gasp as I see the burned and crumbled buildings, the uprooted trees, the huge cracks in the earth. Our own house now has a two-inch crack that runs along the entire floor.

Mother gets up and walks away while the rest of us assess each other's injuries. My cut leg does not look so bad in the light. The bleeding stopped long ago. Grandmother Benu has a cut above her eyes and many bruises. We all have bruises. But no bones are broken and we are still alive.

I find a broken pot which has gathered rain water and we all drink. My body sucks the liquid as if I am a sponge. Then I search through the jumbled mess and find some fruit, and my family and I eat hungrily.

All except Mother, who stands in the corner before Jamila's cupboard and cries as she picks up a piece of broken pottery which Jamila made for her. I sigh. Even now, can she not forget? Can she not see those who live around her? Are we not as important as the dead?

As we finish the fruit, a neighbor comes to our door and inquires about our condition and tells us that his family survived. Then he tells us the prophet wants us to gather at the temple to pray. These words pull my mother's attention from Jamila's corner, and rekindle my anger. Should we pray because of the destruction? The dead? The pain and suffering? The fear?

As I follow my family toward the temple, I cannot keep my eyes from the scene around me. Some houses are like ours, shaken and broken but still standing. Others have fallen, and I see not how any inside could have survived. The house which I saw fall into the earth has disappeared and I see no trace of it, as if it never existed.

The earth trembles beneath my feet and my heart races, yet it only lasts a few moments. I force myself to walk again afterwards despite my fear.

I see my friend and she is crying and I start to go to her, to comfort her, but Mother calls me back. "Not now, Safiya," she says. "You are always rushing off to help others, but this is not the time. Your concern should be with your family."

Father walks before me holding my brother by the hand. Mother follows him. Grandmother Benu stumbles over the rubble that used to be the road and I catch her arm. She smiles at me and pats my shoulder. "My beautiful Safiya," she says.

She often says such things to be kind, but I know I am not so beautiful as Jamila. Or so smart. Or so pure and sweet. I had only to look at Jamila and I could sense the important things she could have done had she lived. But she will do none of them now, for God took her away. I know Omner must often look at me and wish she were back, for I am not as good as she was. Surely he wishes he were still to wed the truly beautiful Jamila.

To forget, I turn my eyes back to the destruction and search the growing crowd for some sign of Omner. Surely he survived, for he is a righteous man. Jamila's death did not weaken his faith. Rather his faith seems somehow stronger because of it.

On the temple grounds, I watch a little neighbor girl run after a butterfly, but before she has run far, she glances back fearfully at her parents, as if she is afraid the earth will shake again.

I hear a voice, but I cannot tell from whence it comes or hear the words. It is a quiet voice, but not the same as the voice of Christ which I heard before. Whoever speaks, my very limbs begin to quake in response to the sound, as if the earth's shaking now moved within my own flesh.

I look around. Mother has stopped, and so has everyone around us. I hear the voice a second time, and my parents do, too.

"Who is saying that?" Mother asks. Her face has gone white and her eyes wide with fear.

The third time I look toward heaven, for I realize now that is from whence the voice comes. But this time I can hear the words which are spoken.

"Behold my Beloved Son, in whom I am well pleased, in whom I have glorified my name--hear ye him."

The voice of God. Can it be? I instinctively drop to my knees and bow my head. Fear fills my heart. My mother kneels beside me. Father pulls my brother into his arms. I hear the rustle of Grandmother's skirts as she kneels slowly behind us.

Again my mind is flooded with fears of what God might do to one so angry at Him and at His Son. I know not what is to come, but my fear pins me to the ground.

Yet my eyes are drawn upward. I see an angel descending from the heavens surrounded by glowing, radiating, warming light. Tears of fear choke me.

The angel wears beautiful white clothes that shine like the sun. I look around and see that everyone is kneeling and gazing into Heaven. Surely everyone in the land of Bountiful can see Him. Are they all drawn to this angel as I am? There is a force about Him that pulls at my heart.

All is quiet while the angel descends. No one speaks a word. Then finally the angel's feet touch the ground in front of the temple and not so far from us.

The angel stretches forth his hand and begins to speak and instantly I recognize the voice. "Behold, I am Jesus Christ, whom the prophets testified shall come into the world; and I have drunk out of that bitter cup which the Father hath given me, and have glorified the Father in taking upon me the sins of the world, in the which I have suffered the will of the Father in all things from the beginning."

Is this truly Jesus who stands but a few feet in front of me? Terror strikes me. Surely He will see my wicked anger and will now punish me for it.

I hear a man crying beside me. When I look, I am amazed for I have never seen my big, strong Father cry before. Yet there he is, kneeling on the ground, gazing toward Jesus, his broad shoulders shuddering with his sobs. I cry, as well, but my tears are from fear.

When Jesus speaks again, His voice strikes to my very center, and I tremble with my fear and amazement. "Arise and come forth unto me," He says, "that ye may thrust your hands into my side, and also that ye may feel the prints of the nails in my hands, and in my feet, that ye may know that I am the God of Israel, and the God of the whole earth, and have been slain for the sins of the world."

My sins have slain Him. And now He is here to exact His punishment upon me.

Still crying, Mother lifts herself up and helps Grandmother Benu to her feet. My body shakes so terribly that I cannot stand. Father puts a hand under my arm and helps me up. A look of joy fills his face. I am not surprised, for Father is a good man, and not wicked as I am.

Now the crowd around us pushes us toward Jesus. No one else hesitates. No one else wants to flee. But I cannot go toward Christ. I cannot. As the crowd pushes me forward, I want to cry out, "NO!", but I cannot for what would the others think? I see people kneeling and kissing Jesus' feet in worship. I see them touching His hands and His feet and His side. I hear them weeping, and their cries find an echo in my soul.

Jesus will only have to look at me to know what is in my heart. He will see the anger there and condemn me before my family and the entire village. I struggle to hold my place, to resist the movement of the crowd, but as the wave of people presses me forward, as each person sees Him and moves on, I am carried closer.

Everyone is so near, they will hear His condemnation of me, will hear His words proclaiming me a wretched sinner. I catch sight of Omner in the crowd to my left, but, just as I am about to call to him, I realize, to my horror, that we will reach Jesus at nearly the same time. Either Jesus will destroy me, or Omner will hear Jesus' condemnation and will no longer want to marry one so wicked as I. My tears flow again. Any small love Omner feels for me will wither and die.

Every wicked thought which I have hidden in my heart will be revealed to all. Then this vengeful God will punish me.

I try to push away from Him, but the people behind me prevent my escape back. My panic rises, but I cannot stop my forward movement.

The crowd pushes me closer until finally I stand before Christ. I look at the prints of the nails on His feet. My stomach tightens at the sight where a huge nail has pierced. How He must have suffered.

I look farther up and see His hands, and the prints in His hands make the tears start in my eyes. I lift my gaze as far as His shoulders and try to prepare myself for His words of condemnation, but I cannot look into the eyes of the Son of God. My breath barely comes and my heart races and my body is cold with my fear.

The crowd pauses as if waiting for me. Shivering, I look up into His eyes. Beautiful, loving eyes. There is no anger here. No hatred. No vengeance. Only an incredible love that shines forth and eases my pain and my anger. A warmth radiates from Him that comforts my very soul.

My shivering stops. And I am still, because as I look at Jesus' face, I remember Him. I remember Him holding me in His arms before I lived here. I remember Him being with our Father in Heaven. I remember His great love for us, and I remember Him offering to come to earth to be our Savior.

And the love that allowed Him to do all this flows from His eyes. I know He sees inside my very heart, and can see my wickedness. I am not worthy to be in His presence. I have been angry with One who loves me more than I know how to love. I have feared One who suffered and died for me. I have forgotten the truth and let my bitterness blind me.

Falling to my knees, I cry out, "I have been wicked, My Lord. Forgive me."

With a gentle hand, Christ helps me to my feet. "Rise, my sister. Feel the prints of the nails in my hands, that ye may know that I am the God of Israel."

My tears fall as I take His hand and see the print of the nail. My heart aches for the pain He went through for all of us. For *me*.

"I have been angry with you," I whisper. "I have been bitter toward our Father."

"Thine anger grew from the pain at losing Jamila. Yet she lives with our Father, and does His work."

"But what of the work she was to do here?" The words tumble from my heart. "She was so righteous and obedient. She could have done so many great and wonderful things."

"That work was never hers to do," He says gently. "You have brought comfort to so many of my children and this is a talent with which our Father has blessed you. As Omner was meant for you, so this great and wonderful work is yours to accomplish. Ease thy mind, Safiya."

He remembers my name! He knows me as well as I know Him. My heart sings with loving warmth.

Still my guilt will not let me stop. "I do not know how I can make amends. Surely there is some price I yet need pay."

His eyes soften and warm, loving energy pulses through me. "Are you truly sorry?"

"Yes, My Lord."

"Are you angry at me still?"

I shake my head and whisper, "You know I am not."

He smiles gently. "Did you think Our Father expects you to be perfect? Perfection is a journey, Safiya, on which you are just now embarking. *I* have already paid the price for you, my dear sister. You need only do your best to obey our Father's will. I have done the rest for you. For this reason came I into the world."

153

He reaches out and places one of His hands with the marks of His death onto my shoulder.

"But I have been so wicked," I begin.

"Do not refuse my gift, Safiya," Christ says. "Accept what I have done for you."

My soul sings with joy yet I cannot stop my tears. My Savior remembers me, understands me, and loves me. And I remember Him.

As I did not want to approach Christ before, now I do not want to leave His side, but others push up to touch Him, and I am swept away.

Behind me, Omner kneels at Christ's feet and worships Him. He has heard me proclaim my wickedness.

I should fear his rejection but, weak from my encounter with this loving Son of a loving Father, I cannot. I rest on the grass in the shade of a tree and I watch as Omner makes his way to me.

He sits before me and takes my hands in his. "I love you," he says.

"And I love you," I whisper.

He rubs my hands gently and tears glisten in his eyes. "I was so frightened you had died in the storm. I could not have borne the pain of your loss. I have *always* loved you, Safiya."

As he looks into my eyes, I see for the first time the love he has is for me, and not for Jamila. Tears of joy fill my eyes. She is where she needs to be. And I am where I need to be.

For the first time since my sister died, I know peace. Christ has worked a miracle--my hurt is gone and my faith restored. Christ's forgiveness is a miracle.

Still holding Omner's hand, I kneel. Omner kneels beside me and together we raise our voices to heaven in a prayer of thanksgiving to our God.

Hosanna to God in the highest. Forever. Amen.

# MORE BONUS MATERIAL

## PREVIEW FROM THE UPCOMING BOOK

# MEN WHO KNEW:
*The Mortal Messiah*

And he said, Go forth,
and stand upon the mountain
before the Lord.
And, behold, the Lord *passed by*,
and a great and strong wind
rent the mountains,
and brake in pieces the rocks
before the Lord;
but the Lord was not in the wind.
And after the wind an earthquake;
but the Lord was not
in the earthquake.
And after the earthquake a fire;
but the Lord was not in the fire.
And after the fire a still small voice.
*(1ˢᵗ Kings 19:11-12)*

And He saw them toiling in rowing;
for the wind was contrary unto them;
and about the fourth watch
of the night
He cometh unto them,
walking upon the sea,
and would have *passed by* them.
*(Mark 6:48)*

# A LITTLE FAITH
## *Peter Walks with Christ*

$T$he wind shrieks about me and I cling to the
rope tied around me to keep from being swept
overboard. It has been thus most of the night.

I am Peter and I take another turn rowing, for the
wind goes against us. I grasp the wooden oar in both
hands and pull with all my strength.

Andrew, whose turn it is to rest, falls back
exhausted against the side of the boat and strains to
fill his lungs with something besides water. He tangles
his arm in the ropes, as well, to anchor himself.

We row in rhythm, fighting with our feet and legs
to stay upright when the big waves hit our ship, one
after another, every few seconds, wave after wave.

Even as we fight to stay afloat, the shriek of the
wind and the howl of the waves grows louder.

Why did Jesus constrain us to get into the ship
and go to the other side, unto Bethsaida and
Capernaum? After He sent away the people who
would have taken Him by force to make Him a King,
even that same five thousand He fed with the five
loaves and the two fishes, He went into the mountain
without us. Who now will bring Him across to us?

I know not.

The more pressing question is if we will make it
through this night with our ship and our lives intact.

I have seen storms before. The other apostles--many of whom are seasoned fishermen, like unto myself--have battled their share of storms, and brought ships in safely despite the waves and wind.

But only one other time have any of us seen waves like these, clawing at the ship as though to drag us under into a watery grave. Wind that howls like a wild beast hungry for our flesh. Only this night we are on our own. Our Lord is not here to command the waves and the winds to be still.

I shiver as the wind chills my skin. I shiver from the fear that has settled deep within my chest. I shiver from the wetness from the waves and my work of rowing as I pull the oars in rhythm with the others. Pull. Lift. Pull. Lift.

*Pull.*

*Lift.*

We are relatively young men, in our prime, but this storm is punishing us and pushing us to our limits.

I do not think we can survive for much longer without sinking.

If only our Lord were here with us. He could calm the storm, as He did once before.

We have rowed five and twenty furlongs, maybe thirty, fighting the wind and the waves with every pull of the oars, yet we seem no closer to shore. At this rate, we will sink before we reach solid land.

The sky is dark except for bursts of lightning that illuminate the sky. Clouds bunch and move and shift, as though they are waves of the sky.

This is the fourth watch of the night, during the time when the night sky begins to lighten with the dawn, yet we will see no sunrise today, I fear.

My turn to row over, I stumble to the place where Andrew had lain, gasping for breath and taking my turn at clinging to the ropes to keep from being swept overboard. Water sloshes around me on the deck. Water slaps my face and tries to snatch my breath. Water clings to me and tries to pull me from the ship.

Finally, having caught my breath, I struggle to my feet to see if there is any break in the clouds, yet I see none. Only waves higher than our ship, halfway up our mast. I have seen many storms in my years as fisherman, but the sight before me chills my heart.

When lightning flashes again, I see a figure walking on the water. I cry out with fear, as do the others.

"It is a spirit," we cry together, of one mind in our fear, our combined voices barely heard.

My soul is sore troubled as the sky begins to lighten--strangely, for there is still no sun. But I can now see the figure clearly, striding upon the waves as though a man walking upon earth that heaves to and fro.

Straightway upon our seeing the spirit, it speaks.

"Be of good cheer," the welcome voice of our Master comes, relieving our fear somewhat. "It is I. Be not afraid."

Our Master? Walking upon the waters? How is this possible?

I wait for Him to calm the waves and the wind, but He does not speak again, only stands on the surface of the roiling waters.

A strange mixture of fear and excitement fills me. My heart burns within me, a desire to join my Lord, no matter how high the waves. I know it is my Lord and I also know I cannot walk on water without His command--but if Jesus commands me to walk on the waves, then He also commands the waves to hold my weight. He could command the water to firm beneath my feet. "Lord, if it be thou, bid me come unto thee on the water."

And through the darkness, I see Jesus's face clearly, and He smiles upon me. "Come."

The other apostles are silent behind me, but perhaps they cannot yell loud enough to be heard above the wind. Clinging to the ropes, I pay them no mind, my focus now only on Jesus. I am astounded. He walks upon the waters. He commands the elements and they obey. He commands me and I obey.

I hold tight to the boat as it continues to pitch and roll, as I throw my legs over the side, and climb down the outside of the boat, all without taking my eyes from Jesus. When my feet touch the surface of the waves, His smile urges me on, as if He is pleased with me.

My heart is full of fear, but I look into the eyes of my Savior and feel His love for me and His pleasure with my decision. A great calm comes over me as I look upon His face and know He has commanded the waves to hold me.

And they do! I take a step and the water holds firm beneath my feet. Another step. A third.

*I am walking upon the water!* I am walking toward my Lord and Master. My heart rejoices in that which I could not do without Jesus.

He stands still while I walk toward Him, as though watching a tottering babe, which I am. A tottering babe upon the waves. A tottering babe in the ways of faith required to walk on water.

Yet a tottering babe daring to take a step. Joy fills my heart.

A wave slaps against me and I hear the roar of the wind that drives the waves before it. I still walk upon the water, but now I raise my hands as if to shield myself. I watch for the next wave . . . and I begin to sink.

My fear returns. My feet are covered with water. My ankles. My knees. The water is pulling me down, as it has fought to do for hours. Though I am a strong swimmer, I could not swim back to the boat. I will drown, no matter how far I could swim in calm water. I cry out for help. "Lord, save me."

Immediately Jesus stretches forth His hand, and catches my arm and pulls me up, my feet once again resting on the surface. He shakes His head and says, "O thou of little faith, wherefore didst thou doubt?"

But I feel no reproach in His words. He merely states the truth: I had only a little faith and so I began to sink. Still I feel His pleasure that I had enough faith--smaller than a mustard seed though it may be--to get out of the boat, to walk thus far. My fear leaves me as I stare into the eyes of Jesus, who smiles at me again.

And then, together, we walk back to the ship, my Master and I, upon the waves. With Him beside me, I can do anything. With Christ, truly all things are possible.

And, when we are come into the ship, the wind ceases. In an instant, the boisterous wind calms. Without the wind, the waves disappear. The dark clouds lighten and part and the rays of the sun ready to be born tint the sky with faint color.

And I am amazed. Obviously, Jesus commanded the wind to cease, as He commanded the waves to hold me. But He did not command it to cease until after I walked with Him on the waves.

Why? He often teaches in parables. Perhaps He has taught us with a living parable this night: It is during the storms of life where we must find the faith to walk with Christ. To learn He will buoy us up and keep us safe and bring us safely home, and reward our efforts.

I know not how, but immediately the ship is at the land whither we were going.

The apostles are amazed beyond measure and wonder, as am I, that our Lord walked upon the waves. I am amazed, as are they, that one of us also walked upon the waves, if only for a moment. They are amazed, as am I, that our ship could immediately reach shore.

The others join me in worshiping our Lord. "Of a truth, thou art the Son of God."

I look at my Lord again, and He smiles at me, pleased with my faulty performance.

As am I. I may be of little faith, still I am the only one with faith enough to climb from the boat and take a step.

I feared, yet still I stepped forth upon the waves.

It seemed not possible, yet I stepped forth upon the waves.

I asked to hear my Master's command, and I stepped forth upon the waves.

I will remember this night forever, and my soul will rejoice in the remembering.

*I walked upon the water with my Lord!*

# *BIBLIOGRAPHY*

JAMES E. TALMAGE, *Jesus The Christ*. Salt Lake City, Utah: Deseret Book Company, 1973.

READER'S DIGEST EDITORS, *Jesus and His Times*. Pleasantville, N.Y.: The Reader's Digest Association, Inc., 1987.

BASED ON LECTURES BY LYDIA MOUNTFORD (Stenographically Recorded), *Jesus In His Homeland*. Pioneer Press.

HARRY EMERSON FOSDICK, *The Man From Nazareth*. New York: Harper and Brothers, 1949.

BRUCE R. McCONKIE, *The Mortal Messiah* - From Bethlehem to Calvary - Book I. Salt Lake City: Deseret Book Company, 1979.

PAUL L. MAIER, *Pontius Pilate*. Grand Rapids, Michigan: Kregel, 1995.

THOMAS M. MUMFORD, *Horizontal Harmony of the Four Gospels in Parallel Columns*. Salt Lake City: Deseret Book Company, 1976.

*The Holy Bible - Authorized King James Edition*. Salt Lake City, Utah: The Church of Jesus Christ of Latter-Day Saints, 1979.

*The Book of Mormon - Another Testament of Jesus Christ*. Salt Lake City, Utah: The Church of Jesus Christ of Latter-Day Saints, 1989.

SHERRILYN KENYON (WITH HAL BLYTHE AND CHARLIE SWEET), *Character-Naming Sourcebook*. Cincinnati, Ohio: Writer's Digest Books, 1994.

NIBLEY, HUGH, *Lehi in the Desert & The World of the Jaredites*. Salt Lake City: Bookcraft, 1952, 1980.

L.D.S. HYMN BOOK

# ABOUT THE AUTHOR

Heather Horrocks traveled the globe for seventeen years with her oilman father, mother and sisters-- moving from South America to the Middle East and back again, with shorter jaunts to other countries tossed in just for fun.

Though she never lived in Israel, she did visit the Holy Land in her youth. She attended junior high and high school on both sides of the Arabian/Persian Gulf (the gulf name changed depending on whether she was living in Kuwait or Iran, and her mail had to reflect that).

After returning to the United States (which she loves wholeheartedly after seeing so much of the rest of the world), she raised a bunch of wonderful kids (whom she loves with all her heart) and started writing and teaching writing (which she also loves). She lives with her husband and true love, Mark, in Salt Lake City with the three children still at home.

Today, as her grown-up babies are leaving home, she has many book-babies ready to be born (some with a decade-long gestation period, poor things).

In her books, she shares the message of Jesus and the healing power of His Atonement. WOMEN WHO KNEW: *The Mortal Messiah* is truly the book of her heart.

Word Garden Press

"Where Good Books Are Always Blossoming"

P.O. Box 27208
Salt Lake City, Utah 84127-0208

Visit our web page at
www.WomenWhoKnew.com
for updates on
new releases.

New books in the
Women Who Knew / Men Who Knew series.

The "I Am Able" Fables
featuring
Suzie Q-That-Stands-For-Wonderful.

# QUICK ORDER FORM

To order more copies of
WOMEN WHO KNEW: *The Mortal Messiah*,
log on to www.WomenWhoKnew.com
or send this form and payment to:

Word Garden Press
P.O. Box 27208
Salt Lake City, Utah 84127-0208

Name: _____

Address: _____

City _____ State _____ Zip _____

Telephone: _____

email address: _____

**Cost:**
$12.95 for Women Who Knew: *The Mortal Messiah*
Please email or write for information on quantity
discounts.

**Sales Tax:**
Please add 6.60% for products shipped to Utah
addresses.

**Shipping by air:**
US: $4 for 1st book and $2 for each additional book.
International: $9 for 1st book; $5 for each additional
book (estimate).